Essays on Confe

Interpreting

Full details of all our publications can be found on http://www.multilingual-matters.com, or by writing to Multilingual Matters, St Nicholas House, 31–34 High Street, Bristol BS1 2AW, UK.

Essays on Conference Interpreting

James Nolan

MULTILINGUAL MATTERS
Bristol • Blue Ridge Summit

DOI https://doi.org/10.21832/NOLAN7994
Library of Congress Cataloging in Publication Data
A catalog record for this book is available from the Library of Congress.
Names: Nolan, James - author.
Title: Essays on Conference Interpreting/James Nolan.
Description: Bristol, UK; Blue Ridge Summit: Multilingual Matters,
  [2020]. | Includes bibliographical references and index. | Summary:
  "This book, drawing on the author's 30-year career, seeks to define what
  constitutes good interpreting and how to develop the skills and
  abilities that are conducive to it. It places interpretation in its
  historical context and examines the uses and limitations of modern
  technology for interpreting"—Provided by publisher.
Identifiers: LCCN 2019049205 (print) | LCCN 2019049206 (ebook) |
  ISBN 9781788927987 (paperback) | ISBN 9781788927994 (hardback) |
  ISBN 9781788928007 (pdf) | ISBN 9781788928014 (epub) | ISBN 9781788928021
  (kindle edition) Subjects: LCSH: Simultaneous interpreting. | Congresses and
  conventions—Translating services. | Translating and interpreting. |
  Translating and interpreting—Study and teaching. | Translating and
  interpreting—Technological innovations. | Language and culture.
Classification: LCC P306.95.N583 2020 (print) | LCC P306.95 (ebook) |
  DDC 418/.02—dc23 LC record available at https://lccn.loc.gov/2019049205
LC ebook record available at https://lccn.loc.gov/2019049206

British Library Cataloguing in Publication Data
A catalogue entry for this book is available from the British Library.

ISBN-13: 978-1-78892-799-4 (hbk)
ISBN-13: 978-1-78892-798-7 (pbk)

Multilingual Matters
UK: St Nicholas House, 31–34 High Street, Bristol BS1 2AW, UK.
USA: NBN, Blue Ridge Summit, PA, USA.

Website: www.multilingual-matters.com
Twitter: Multi_Ling_Mat
Facebook: https://www.facebook.com/multilingualmatters
Blog: www.channelviewpublications.wordpress.com

The policy of Multilingual Matters/Channel View Publications is to use papers that are
natural, renewable and recyclable products, made from wood grown in sustainable
forests. In the manufacturing process of our books, and to further support our policy,
preference is given to printers that have FSC and PEFC Chain of Custody certification.
The FSC and/or PEFC logos will appear on those books where full certification has been
granted to the printer concerned.

Typeset by Nova Techset Private Limited, Bengaluru and Chennai, India.
Printed and bound by CPI Group (UK) Ltd, Croydon, CR0 4YY
Printed and bound in the US by NBN.

Contents

Preface

What we now want is closer contact and better understanding between individuals and communities all over the earth, and the elimination of egoism and pride which is always prone to plunge the world into primeval barbarism and strife. Peace can only come as a natural consequence of universal enlightenment. Nikola Tesla, *My Inventions* (1919)

The art of interpreting springs from an intuitive understanding that, while ideas may be captured in or represented by words, they have a life of their own that extends far beyond the capacity of words to convey. In the perennial debate between translators who advocate 'following the words' and those who advocate 'following the meaning', the interpreter falls squarely in the latter camp.

The interpreter knows that words are like the pebbles arrayed on a beach, displaying variety in number, shape, size and color, but ideas are more like the sea which envelops and shapes those pebbles by its power and motion but extends far beyond the shore into infinity. The simultaneous interpreter striving to grasp and transform a stream of words and ideas knows that he is being 'asked to do something that does not come naturally' and that 'it is the mark of effortful activities that they interfere with each other, which is why it is difficult or impossible to conduct several at once.'[1]

https://www.freeimages.com/photo/sea-side-1173092

1 Interpreting in the Global Arena[2]

Interpretation can be defined in a nutshell as conveying understanding. Its value stems from the fact that a speaker's meaning is best expressed in his or her native language but is best understood in the languages of the listeners. Human speech, consisting of sounds, can instantly convey a vast range of ideas, nuances and feelings, not all of which can be captured or represented in writing. Some emotive aspects of a spoken message are conveyed even if one does not understand the language being spoken, provided the speech is audible and there is some variability in the volume and pitch perceived. Just as a printed score is only a symbolic graphic representation of a song or musical composition, a written translation is only a written record of the author's thoughts using a different set of symbols. The intensity, subtlety, range and ephemeral nature of human speech challenges our ability to memorialize it in a form that can be transformed into different languages. The interpreter's specialty is rendering speech into a different language immediately, before it fades from memory.

Through the art of interpretation several complex interrelated processes converge to convey the semantic and emotive meaning of a message from one language and culture to another. The interaction of these processes and the difficulty of coordinating them simultaneously in the oral/aural mode (or in sign language) require attention,[3] sensitivity, concentration and mental agility. In some ways, training for interpreting resembles training for musicianship or acting: the most fruitful approach is guided practice, individual aptitudes and skills are important, talent needs to be nurtured and encouraged, performance is improved by awareness of audience expectations, intuition plays a role, and there may be several valid ways of interpreting a particular passage or speech. The skills required for interpretation, especially simultaneous interpretation, must be developed through practice to the point where they become automatic. The reason for this is ably explained by psychologist Michael Gazzaniga in his lecture 'The Interpreter,' delivered at the University of Edinburgh on 15 October 2009,[4] which may be viewed online.

A discussion of interpreting today must begin by putting the topic in historical perspective. Contemporary societies are in the midst of a technological transition known as 'digitalization' which may prove to be the most important technological advance since the invention of printing. Digital media now make it possible to channel and manage contents worldwide in real time, conveying vast volumes of data and knowledge in many languages. Those vast flows are in some ways defined by the means used to convey them.

The phrase 'The medium is the message' was introduced in Marshall McLuhan's book *Understanding Media: The Extensions of Man*, published in 1964. McLuhan proposed that communication is marked by the medium carrying it as much as by the content carried. He said that a medium affects the society in which it plays a role not only by the content delivered over the medium, but also by the characteristics of the medium itself. The speed and efficiency of the analog media described by McLuhan (e.g. television, cinema) has been increased many times over by advances in electronic communications and digitalization. From the emergence of writing and printing during the first millennium of human history through the development of analog media during the second millennium, we now see the emergence of an era of digital media at the beginning of the third millennium, with implications for translation and interpretation and the way they are now performed.

Interpretation must be understood as an art which plays an important role in human history, not merely as a messaging function. Translation stretches the boundaries of a natural language by introducing new ideas and values that must be named in order to be referred to and discussed, and that 'stretching exercise' leaves a language richer, stronger and more vigorous than it was before.

As noted by Professor Juliane House, 'Translation is a particular kind of intercultural communication aimed at intercultural understanding. Intercultural understanding is closely related to the most important concept in translation theory: <u>functional equivalence</u>. It can be achieved when a translation has a function in the target culture comparable to the function its original has in its cultural context.'[5] However, because functional equivalence is rarely exact, it forces the mind of the listener or reader to think outside the box of his/her language, introducing an element of cognitive value added.

Because mechanical methods of translation can only use the words and rules that have been built into them, they fail to yield the added value that arises from the cognitive stretching exercise. They may display a degree of accuracy and efficiency but they lack the necessary breadth, empathy, originality and creativity to deal with a natural language, which is arguably the single most complex system known to the human mind.[6]

Until recently, all translation was understood to be performed by people. Now, situations arise in which the need is felt to spell out that we are referring to 'human translation' because verbally encoded outputs of computer algorithms are being produced and marketed as translations. See, e.g.: 'The fact that translation is a largely invisible activity is not a problem per se; firms and administrations working in an international context still use it daily. On the other hand, the Directorate General of Translation (DGT) at the European Commission (and many experts and professionals that we contacted for this study), believe that by constantly remaining in the background, translation and **especially human and professional translation** may eventually be perceived as a superfluous activity, a cost that is not necessarily justified. If this perception were to spread among the citizens of Europe it could rapidly become a threat to European multilingualism, for which the translation activities in European institutions provide a solid base.'[7]

Some of the products of automation can be made to mimic self-conscious human thought and to parrot human speech so convincingly that the effect is like finding a genie in a magic lantern and we could almost forget that what we are hearing is synthesized verbalization rather than articulated thought. People are becoming accustomed at an early age to rely on a portable electronic device to carry out tasks of daily living to an extent that can isolate them and de-sensitize them to what is happening around them, compounding the intercultural opacity between speakers of different languages that is commonly referred to as 'the language barrier'.

The word 'translator' is sometimes being loosely used by analogy in reference not to people but to devices that are in fact electronic phrase-books structured to retrieve equivalent entries or pre-recorded phrases[8] in a manner similar to the pre-recorded 'guides' that one can rent at some museums or zoos. Some public authorities reluctant to invest in language education and professional translation training are taking the easy way out by treating computer coding as a 'language' that students may opt to study in school in lieu of a second language.[9] For similar reasons, complex computerized security protocols are being introduced into the process of providing language access in public services and in procedures for training and testing linguistic personnel, burdening practitioners in the belief that mechanical measures can substitute competence and integrity or safeguard against hackers. More seriously, the pervasive temptation to give in to convenience and 'let the computer do it' is hampering well-rounded education, depriving students of a range of benefits:

Learning a foreign language has benefits that reach beyond the ability to communicate effectively with people from other cultures. Mirta Desir, founder and CEO of Smart Coos, points to the benefits of being both bilingual and bi-literate, saying, 'Biliteracy and bilingualism have a profound effect on the brain, improving cognitive skills not related to language.'

The American Council on the Teaching of Foreign Languages found that learning a foreign language supports academic achievement and provides the following benefits:

- higher scores on standardized tests
- increased development of student reading ability
- transfer of skill from one language to another
- increased linguistic awareness

- increased ability of scientific hypothesizing
- offset of age-related cognitive losses
- increased problem-solving ability.

While those benefits are applicable across virtually all academic endeavors, access to classes to learn foreign languages is lacking in the American system of education.[10]

There is a need to define more carefully what we mean by 'language', what is meant by translation/interpretation,[11] the nature and scope of the non-utilitarian functions it performs, and what role can or should be played by technology. Thought should also be given in this context to the hidden costs of xenophobia and nationalism in a globalized world, which can make enforced monolingualism a false economy.

With the advent of globalization we found ourselves living in a global village. Now, with the digital revolution and advances in cyber-engineering, we are moving towards a digital global village, one whose clearest external manifestation is the Internet, a virtual world that reflects an even greater and older one: 'When you access the vast global network of computers we call the Internet, you can travel the world, find information, and interact with people in a way that was never before possible. The creation of the net was an awesome leap in technological evolution. Yet, for all that it offers, it is the merest shadow of something much larger and much older. Language is the real information highway, the first virtual world. Language is the worldwide web, and everyone is logged on.'[12]

In the process, we are automating and computerizing a growing number of human activities and mimicking human faculties and cultural features or memes, sometimes without regard to whether the human element of the activity constitutes its essence and makes it a suitable or unsuitable candidate for automation or mechanical replication. While no one would deny, for example, that the process of packaging pharmaceuticals in a sterile robotic environment untouched by human hands is a useful innovation, the question we now face is whether the process of transferring ideas and feelings between people of different languages and cultures can or should be carried out untouched by human minds. Much as we may appreciate the practical uses of the smartphone, one has to ask how smart it would be to allow a device to begin doing our thinking for us, regardless of how artificially 'intelligent' that device may become. The human brain is still the most powerful 'computer', and the repository of some 300,000 years of evolutionary and historical experience, and it is the awareness of that species-consciousness and cultural heritage that enables a translator or interpreter to extract the correct intended meaning from the context of an utterance in ways that elude even the best MT programs.[13] According to one of the prevailing definitions used by linguists, '...language is not a singular phenomenon or a specific thing. Rather, it is multidimensional – interdependent and interconnected with other human abilities and other cognitive tasks. ... In this view, language is not a monolithic thing that we *have*; rather, it is a thing that we *do*. It arises from the coordination of many genetic settings; these are expressed as a set of physical, perceptual, and conceptual biases that underlie certain abilities and behaviors, all of which allows us to learn language.'[14] If speaking a language is a thing that we *do*, it cannot, by definition, be done by a machine. A similar view expressed by Steven Pinker is that the human language system comprises both a memory-based data-set component compiled from human experience and an algorithmic rule-based component which helps to process the content of the former in producing spoken output. The latter component could theoretically be reproduced in a computer and programmed to independently re-create itself, but the former component could not.[15]

Computers are built to receive, encode, re-encode, re-arrange or transmit strings of words according to a program.[16] A young lady I saw at the supermarket with the word 'HI' printed on the front of her T-shirt and the word 'BYE' printed on the back was using a cultural artifact to send one of two pre-encoded messages, depending on the social syntax created by her location and bodily posture. What a computer does is more complex but not different in kind, and this kind of communication is remote from what human beings do in expressing thoughts and emotions. Inadequate human control over what a computer is doing with language can wreak havoc with the message in the same way that an automated self-driving car can run amok in normal street traffic because it lacks an actual sensitive awareness of human presence and physical and social context.[17] The rigid protocols required to communicate mechanically or to give instructions to a computer through its user interface tend to suppress normal human emotions and reactions that are a part of communication between human beings and tend to simplistically reduce all situations and decisions to binary choices. The very process of conveying messages by data-entry while using a keyboard favors a static frame of mind and tends to filter out expressive or emotive content.

See also: Stephen Budianski. 'Lost in Translation'. *The Atlantic*, December 1998.

https://www.freeimages.com/search/person-keyboarding

https://www.freeimages.com/search/woman-gesturing-hand

But not everyone is framing these questions in those terms. For example, a comment in the quarterly journal of the Carolina Interpreters' Association, *CATI Quarterly*, suggested that although we must educate the public not to rely on mobile machine translation apps to tackle serious texts, 'having at one's fingertips the ability to understand another language, even in limited form, is truly a technological marvel.'[18] That is true, but the danger is that, compared with the effort involved in learning a foreign language, many will be content with their language of birth and eager to jump on the cybernetic bandwagon and 'let the computer do it', so that fewer people will learn to speak a second language well enough to interpret it. Thus, for example, reports have surfaced about attempts to market what are purported to be automated electronic interpretation devices[19] analogous to those used for draft machine translation of expository texts.

When translating large texts which are mainly expository, descriptive or formulaic ('boilerplate') it is now possible to use revised and post-edited automated translations in order to deal with voluminous material whose contents is structured according to rules of logic that can be incorporated into computer algorithms. If most of the meaning of a work can be derived from words, automated translation can produce useful drafts. So, for example, it is reported that an artificial intelligence program developed by the French team of Quantmetry and Deepl has successfully translated an 800-page reference work entitled *Deep Learning* from English into French in only 12 hours, producing text of heretofore unprecedented quality for a machine translation (October 2018).[20]

Such machine translation does not produce satisfactory results with writing that presents stylistic challenges, such as poetry, drama or oratory, or when a technical/scientific piece of writing departs from the expository and makes use of literary devices or allusions, or calls for imagination, insight, persuasiveness, advocacy, or skill in 'reading between the lines.' For example, Barbara Lovett Cline's essay *An Introduction to Modern Quantum Theory* makes use of a classical literary device: a fictional dialogue between two imaginary scientists, named 'Oldfield' and 'Newcomb,' to contextualize some new insights about quantum physics. The Spanish version of this essay, translated by Juan Almela, names the two fictional characters 'Torrevieja' and 'Casanova'. The translator's literary input or poetic license shows through here, as the names he creates encapsulate the idea of an old bastion and a new house of learning. Such imaginative re-interpretation is beyond the capacity of machine translation.[21]

Recently, the machine translation interest group represented on the ASTM sub-committee that the author collaborated with to create a Standard Guide for Language Interpretation[22] went so far as to suggest that 'machine interpretation' would replace 50% of human interpretation within five years. If telephone interpreting of simple messages via MT is included in the figures, that could turn out to be true in a statistical sense.

But if it does, can the 50% of the work done by machines that are not self-aware be described as 'interpretation'?[23]

Several of the routine clerical functions that go into the preparation of documents and into making and publishing translations can be performed more quickly and cheaply by computer-assisted methods, e.g. compiling and alphabetizing terminology, storing and retrieving terms or segments of text such as quotations and boilerplate provisions, looking up possible synonyms, fact-checking from online sources, doing word counts and frequency counts, performing document-review tasks such as identifying and counting the occurrence of given terms or references in a voluminous document, etc. But recently the view has gained ground that translation can itself be performed by computers, a far-fetched idea resulting in errors that may prompt prohibition of its use for rendering official documents. In India, in the wake of machine translation errors, government authorities have banned the use of a popular online MT program: 'It's official now. Google is not the answer to everything under the sun. Not, at least, in Maharashtra. The BJP-led government in the state has barred its officers and employees from using Google's popular translation tool for rendering official documents in other languages. The ban, imposed through an official notification on Monday, comes in the wake of a major embarrassment to the state government over a faulty translation of a circular for imposing sedition charges.'[24]

What most machine-translation developments have in common is a failure to recognize that the activity they propose to automate is not a pastime or a computer game but arguably the world's oldest vocation, one whose traceable origins in recorded history go back to about 3000 BC in Egypt, 2600 B.C. in Mesopotamia and 165 B.C. in China[25] and whose practitioners have often enjoyed official status and professional prestige by virtue of the important role they fulfilled. At one point in history, Isaac Asimov, a prominent scientific historian, considers translation to have been vital to science: 'The twelfth century is unique in the history of science as being the time when it was possible for translation to be the most important scientific work. The books of the Arabic scholars who for centuries had preserved the works of the Greek philosophers by translation and commentary, began to be rendered into Latin.'[26]

Nearly as old as the practice of translation is the debate over how translation is best done, i.e. whether the translator should follow the words or follow the meaning. 'The first Western writers to leave a record of their approach to translation are Cicero and Horace. Both were part of the Roman tradition of using the practice of translation as a means to expand the literary domain by translating Greek works, which were the local favorites, into Latin. These two men exerted an enormous influence on translation strategies for centuries because they preferred what they referred to as a strategy focusing on the meaning, by contrast with a more literal or word-for-word translation. Marcus Tullius Cicero

(106–43 BC) was a Roman writer, politician, lawyer and translator, whose work *De optimo genere oratorum* (46 BC) sets out his approach to translation. In this introduction to one of his own translations, Cicero explains that he avoids the Latin tradition then favored of presenting translations word for word alongside the Greek original, as he preferred "a language in keeping with our own usage" since, he said, "if I translate word for word, the result will sound clumsy." Horace (Quintus Horatius Flaccus, 65–8 BC) agreed with Cicero, and in *Ars Poetica* (circa 20 BC) he too takes a stand against translation that copies "the original word for word, like an enslaved translator". For Horace, the aesthetic quality of a translation had to take precedence over fidelity to the original.'[27] Horace's opinion reminds us of the importance political power has always had in the development of translation as an art or craft in times when only the cultured or educated classes had the resources to acquire a second language.

Photo courtesy of Leiden National Museum of Antiquities – Believed to be the earliest known depiction of an interpreter at work, this Egyptian bas-relief showing a detail of a very large frieze from the tomb of Haremhab (or Horemhab) at Saqqara, ancient Memphis, just outside Cairo, dates from about 1330 BCE. Today the frieze is in the National Antiquities Museum at Leiden, Netherlands. [Collection data and images from the National Museum of Antiquities are freely available for reuse by developers under a Creative Commons license. Object descriptions (metadata) are available under a CC0 licence. The images (content) are made available under a CC BY licence. This means that you are permitted to copy, adapt, distribute, or perform this material without permission from the National Museum of Antiquities. We would appreciate being mentioned as the source of the material. The correct citation form is: National Museum of Antiquities, Leiden.]

As early as the Ottoman Empire, the profession of interpreter ('dragoman') had taken on a form, content and official status not unlike that of an ambassador or foreign minister:

> Above all, foreign diplomats had to contend with the problem of language. For none knew Turkish, and few Turks ... knew a European language. The foreign envoy thus depended upon his own dragoman –his interpreter and intelligence agent – who was usually a Greek or a Levantine of Latin origin. Acting as his intermediary with the officials of the Porte, the dragoman was in a position, by selective or slanted interpretation, to influence talks as he chose; to further his own interests through calculated leakages to his fellow dragomen and other confederates. But in 1669 this system was rationalized and improved by the creation, for Christian subjects alone whether Greeks or Armenians, of the high office of Dragoman of the Porte. Drawn as a rule from the Greek mercantile community, the Phanariots, his rank amounted in fact to that of a minister of foreign affairs. Around him other responsible official

Interprète du Divan Imp.

From the New York Public Library, George Arents Collection. 'Interprète au divan imp. [18]' The New York Public Library Digital Collections. 1223. http://digitalcollections.nypl.org/items/510d47e3-759f-a3d9-e040-e00a18064a99 – free to use without restriction.

posts were allotted henceforward to Christians, mostly of the Greek Orthodox faith. For Greeks, through their trade, were familiar with the languages of the West, of which the Moslem Turkish elite were in general ignorant, and would send their sons to such Western universities as Padua. In particular, they were to serve often as ambassadors or as governors of autonomous Christian provinces. Thus, with the lapsing of the Sultan's Slave Household, did the Ottomans continue, without either conscription or enforced conversion, to draw on the abilities of their Christian subjects. The work of the Dragoman of the Porte as relations with Europe developed became increasingly arduous. It took the form of regular contacts with foreign envoys, for discussions of their business, his services as interpreter at audiences with the Sultan and interviews with the Grand Vezir; correspondence with foreign governments, which he and his staff had to translate from the Turkish; a perusal of foreign news sheets and similar sources to familiarize his government with European affairs.[28]

The interpreter's role is most conspicuous in international relations, but interpretation is a profession that relies on mental and cultural processes that have been at the core of how civilizations grow and develop as far back as human memory can reach, older in fact than some other professions that could not have developed as they have if language and communication had not developed ahead of them or in parallel with them. Historically, whenever a polity or society has been large enough to encompass two or more languages or cultures, translation/interpretation has served to underpin the authority which held the entity together. Moreover, it is well known that cultures isolated from outside influences tend to stagnate while cultural growth often occurs through cultural borrowing[29] accomplished through translation. Translators and interpreters, acting as the agents of that change, have often been the ones who built the intellectual bridges that enabled something new or useful to enter their cultures from abroad, fostering the cultural growth of a nation or of a domain of science or learning. An example is the reign of King Alfonso the Wise of Castile, who ruled in the period 1252–1284: 'He possessed a spirit of wide tolerance. Most of the learning of the age was locked up in Greek, Latin, Hebrew and Arabic texts. Alfonso's contemporaries had no direct contact with Greek literature and had to be content with such Greek lore as the Arabs had preserved. No religious scruples prevented Alfonso from calling learned Jews and Moors to his court. These he set to work, side by side with Christian monks, translating, popularizing, compiling from diverse sources into encyclopedic works. The significance of the medieval Renaissance is that a considerable portion of ancient and oriental learning was brought within the ken of many unversed in Latin. The circle of readers and thinkers was extended. And from Spain this knowledge passed to the rest of Europe. ...'.[30] By the end of the 15th century, at least 20 works from Arabic were printed in Europe in Latin translations.[31]

Alfonso the Wise
From Wikimedia Commons, free media repository
Alfonso X of Castile, from his Libro de los Juegos (folio 65r)
http://commons.wikimedia.org/wiki/Image:LibroDesJuegasAlfonXAndCourt.jpg

Translation magnifies knowledge by expanding the circle of those who can share and exchange it, thus bringing more individual insights to bear upon it. A good example is medicine, a field of knowledge that has benefited from translation since its earliest times and owes many of its advances to underlying cultural translational processes. A text originally written in Ionic Greek between the third and fourth centuries BC, the Hippocratic Oath, requiring physicians to respect paramount ethical principles, including confidentiality and non-malfeasance, has formed the basis of medical ethics in the Western world ever since and has remained a rite of passage for medical practitioners in many countries down to the present day. By means of translation, this document has in effect served as a template for the creation of basic codes of medical practice in different cultures and civilizations with different languages.[32] With each such translation, medical knowledge has been enriched by the lexical resources, innovations and insights of each adopting language, forming a vibrant and growing body of knowledge.

Yet, in stark contrast with this tradition, the weblog of a US translation agency, commenting on a recent article about European regulations, reported that the pharmaceutical industry sees some translations as 'a waste of paper.'[33] One has to ask: If automation progressed to the point where it became possible to computerize and automate medical consultations or practices ('telemedicine') should we allow that to happen or would we be running the risk of expunging the Hippocratic Oath and neutralizing the capacity for empathy, innovation and compassion that the history of medicine illustrates? And if automation undermines the motivating power of translation/interpretation as a vocation and depletes its

Fragment of the Hippocratic Oath in Ionian Greek, 3rd century Papyrus Oxyrhynchus Wikimedia Commons
https://commons.wikimedia.org/wiki/File:Papyrus_text;_fragment_of_Hippocratic_oath._Wellcome_L0034090.jpg

vigor as a profession and art, that dehumanization may have a similar effect over time on medicine, law,[34] education and other professions and disciplines that translation supports by providing links, forging connections and fostering cross-fertilization. The best translation (written or oral) draws on a deep understanding of human experience and the human condition from which insights and intuitions arise that shape the translation process in a creative way. We should take care to preserve those human insights and intuitions as an essential dimension of the craft of translation, recalling that the portion of the human mind that can reduce human experience to convenient templates and algorithms is only a small part of what the human mind is capable of.

Given the antiquity of language[35] translation and its historical predecessor interpretation must of necessity be ancient skills that were used in rudimentary ways even by 'primitive' peoples.[36] We do not know exactly how old language is,[37] but some anthropologists believe that humans must have developed language even before they discovered fire,[38] and language defined as symbols recorded in a tangible object is believed to be some 300,000 years old.[39] Moreover, regardless of what conclusion one is led to by speculating about language origins, the fact remains that the formation and present distribution of languages and language families in the world indicates that cultures with different languages have coexisted in proximity to each other and influenced each other over a span of thousands of years, so that there must have been contact and communication between them[40] despite language differences. Languages often bear traces of such cross-fertilization that reveal how they helped each other to develop. This did not happen by osmosis but by mimesis, with the words and structures of one serving as a model for the other, consciously or imperceptibly. Although evidence of this process can be found even in the etymologies of many dictionary entries, we do not need a Rosetta Stone to infer that when the speakers of ancient languages entered into contacts with one another, some form of translation or interpretation must have taken place, i.e. some members of the two groups must have first taken pains (and assumed the risks) of acquiring the ability to understand and decode messages from the other group or tribe and to encode messages addressed to the other group. And this must have begun to occur in many humble ways by many anonymous people long before archaeological or written historical records tell us that the Egyptian and Aztec empires evolved castes of interpreters, that the Romans translated the Greek classics into Latin and were inspired by them, or that the Library of Baghdad translated the Western classics into Arabic and preserved them for posterity. Thus, although there may be scant prehistoric records and although the practitioners of the craft worked in the shadows, it is reasonable to hypothesize that the practice of interpreting from one natural language to another is a common practice that is thousands of years old. The skills required to perform that function may even have been more robust and widespread among populations in ancient times than they are today – in our age marked by the more rigid conventions of writing – since communication by speech in preliterate societies was the normal, if not the only, way of communicating: for most of human history communication has meant oral communication and tradition has meant oral tradition.[41] Evidence of this is the relative ease with which indigenous interpreters and guides – those we know of – took to the task of interpreting, without need of special training, when they encountered Europeans in the new world.

In South America, oral translation between indigenous languages that was required for official purposes by Aztec emperors was a function entrusted to a class of professionals.[42] In the Inca empire, the largest of its day after China, the dominant language Quechua was influenced by another indigenous language, Aymara, in the Cuzco region.[43] During the Discovery, interpreters were sent to Europe to learn Spanish in order to be enlisted by Columbus and other explorers in subsequent voyages. They sometimes played more than a linguistic role, acting also as emissaries or missionaries, helping their European employers to consolidate conquests and to spread their laws and religions. A known historical example is that of Enrique, the slave interpreter of Magellan, who was able to communicate with the rulers of the Philippines and to negotiate for Magellan and represent the King of Spain.[44] In North America, Sacajawea, the Shoshone woman who served as interpreter and guide to the Lewis and Clark expedition in 1805 and 1806, rendered her services orally, using her voice and memory to carry out the responsibility of gathering and transferring the vital information that Lewis and Clark needed to survive along their trek, opening the way for the westward expansion of the United States.[45]

Sacagawea interpreting for Lewis and Clark
1905 Painting *Lewis and Clark on the Lower Columbia* (Height: 28 in (71.1 cm); Width: 24 in (60.9 cm)) by Charles Marion Russell; Opaque and transparent watercolor over graphite underdrawing on paper. Source: Humanities Texas. This image is in the public domain due to age. Wikimedia Commons – https://commons. wikimedia.org/wiki/File:Lewis_and_clark-expedition.jpg

Whether the driving force was discovery, conquest, exploration or nation-building, interpreters have been active in the Americas for some 500 years, performing tasks of considerable responsibility for the indigenous and European empires or states that have existed there. Elsewhere in the world, the critical role of interpreters in the social/political structures of their respective societies is also a matter of historical record:

In earliest times ... their bilingual ability was a feature of their family or early life circumstances; they were not products of interpreter training programs. But in Ancient Egypt, a special Egyptian-Greek interpreters' caste was formed; in Ancient Greece, young Persians were instructed in Greek; and in Ancient Rome, bilingual instruction in Latin and Greek was the mark of a cultured citizen. Byzantium had an Office for Barbarians, who learned the customs and languages of the subject peoples in that vast empire. In fourteenth century Toledo, a quadrilingual translation centre flourished in Arabic, Hebrew, Spanish and Latin. The Ottoman Empire established a caste-like institution of dragomen Turks and foreign nationals who conducted interpretation between the Turks and Europeans. In China, civil service examinations of translators and interpreters were set up in ten foreign languages; their positions eventually became hereditary, even though such positions were considered low-status, since the interpreters were required to have contact with despised 'barbarians'.[46]

Since language is a major driving force of human cultures, the contribution translation makes by adding a further dimension or distinct world-view to a given culture at a given time confers a competitive advantage on the culture that cultivates this practice. The practice of translation stretches and expands the code that the human mind uses to think: language. Practicing the art of translation helps a culture to broaden its horizons and to assimilate useful words, ideas, values and insights from other cultures. A good example is the Arab assimilation of Hellenistic ideas engendering a body of knowledge that was known at the time as 'the foreign sciences', thereby acknowledging its origins in translation. An event of primary importance was the penetration of Greek thought into the Baghdad of the early 'Abbasid era. The aptitude of the Arab spirit for absorbing other ideas and its capacity for assimilation here received full scope, and there was a lively enthusiasm for translations of Greek philosophical and scientific works. Even before the coming of Islam, translations from Greek into Syriac were not unusual, and the arrival of Islam was to give rise to many Arabic translations, either through the intermediary of Syriac or directly from Greek. At Baghdad, there were teams of translators, at first Christians, later Muslims, under the patronage of the caliphs. The most famous is that of the Nestorian Hunayn b. Ishaq, his son Ishaq, and his nephew Hubaysh. There was also the Jacobite Qusta b. Luqa, a little later Abu Bishr Matta b. Yunus (a Nestorian), Ibn 'Adi, Yahya b. Bitriq, and others. These groups of translators enriched the Arabic language with works translated from Plato and Aristotle – and from Plotinus confused with Aristotle – from Ptolemy, Galen, Hippocrates and many others besides. The libraries multiplied: among them were the Bayt al-hikma ('House of Wisdom') of the Caliph al-Ma'mun at Baghdad with its many Greek manuscripts, and the Dâr al-kutub ('House of Books') at Basra, with scholarships which students could hold there. A century later Fatimid Cairo was enriched by the huge Palace Library with 18,000 works of 'foreign sciences', and by the Dâr al-'ilm 'House of learning') or Ddr al-hikma founded by al-Hakim in the 4th/10th century. This directly Hellenistic influence, added to the Perso-Greek (and Hindu) contributions of Gondeshapur, produced a whole activity of scientific research in the modern meaning of the word: mathematics, astronomy, physics and chemistry, medicine. Although astronomy was still mixed with astrology and chemistry with alchemy, it was in the Arab and Persian Muslim countries that very remarkable progress was made in science at this time, and for several centuries following. Whole chapters and monographs have been written on Arabian science and its riches are still far from having been fully listed.'[47]

The history of English records how the borrowing of words and ideas from other languages in myriad ways has vastly expanded the corpus of words and ideas that make up the fabric of this rich language. The Christianizing of Britain in 597 brought England into contact with Latin civilization and made significant additions to its vocabulary. The Scandinavian invasion resulted in a considerable mixture of the two races and their languages. The Norman Conquest in 1066 made English the language mainly of the lower classes, while the nobles used French on most occasions. And when English regained its status as the language of all the population it was an English greatly changed in form and vocabulary from what it had been before the conquest.[48] Modern English has borrowed words from some 350 other languages.[49]

Recently, history has returned the favor, enabling English to play the role of a useful online common language or lingua franca among the Nordic countries, Norway, Sweden and Finland: 'Among more than 6,900 languages that are currently in use all over the world, English takes third place for native speakers, after Mandarin and Spanish. There are 1,299 million native Chinese speakers and only 378 million English according to The Statistics Portal. Its usage online reflects different numbers, however. English accounts for 25.4% of all searches, while Chinese influences for 19.3% of actions on the world wide web, and Spanish amounts to only 8.1% of internet usage, according to data from December 2017.' https://t2conline.com/12-fun-facts-about-english/

Geoffrey Chaucer was introduced to the works of Petrarch and Boccaccio on a trip to Italy in 1372. While the author of the Canterbury Tales was not primarily a translator, much of his great classic was adapted from the writings of Italian contemporaries, thus initiating an English poetic tradition of borrowing and adapting. There were in England 43 printed editions of classical works in English translation by the mid-16th century, and 119 such editions before 1600.[50] Some 41% of English words come from French, 15% from Latin, 5% from Old Norse, 1% from Dutch, and only about a third of its words are 'native' English.[51] It is thus no exaggeration to say that the lingua franca which has become so dominant in today's world[52] that it sometimes seems to cast doubt on the need for translation is itself largely a product of translation.[53] A natural language

A N

Annals, are a yearly Chronological Account of the remarkable Events of a State; as the Annals of *Tacitus*.

Annates, (Lat.) firft Fruits paid out of fpiritual Benefices.

Anneal, a Commodity brought from *Barbary*, ufed by Painters and Dyers.

Annealing, a Staining and Baking of Glafs, fo that the Colour may go quite through it.

Annex, (Lat.) to unite or joyn one thing to another.

Annexation, uniting of Lands or Renrs to the Crown.

Annihilation, (Lat.) is a deftroying or turning any created Being into nothing.

Anni nubiles, (Lat.) the Age in which a Maid becomes fit for Marriage, which is at twelve Years.

Anniverfary, that comes every Year at a certain time; Yearly. Alfo the yearly Return of the Day of Death of any Perfon, which the Religious regiftered in their Obitual or Martyrology, and Annually obferved in Gratitude to their Founders and Benefactors.

Anno Dom. (Lat.) fignifies the Year of our Lord.

Annomeans, the Name of the thorough paced *Arians* in the 4th Century, becaufe they held the Effence of the Son of God unlike that of the Father.

Annotation, (Lat.) a Noting or Marking; alfo a Remark, Note, or Obfervation.

A N

Annoyance, (Fr.) Prejudice, Damage, Injury.

Annual, (Lat) of or belonging to the Year, yearly.

Annuates Mufculi, a Pair of Mufcles at the Root of the Tranfverfe *Vertebra* of the Back; called alfo *Recti interni minores*; ferving to nod the Head directly forward.

Annuity, a yearly Rent to be paid for Term of Life or Years.

Annular Cartilage, the Second Griftle of the *Larynx*.

Annular Protuberance, part of the human Brain lying between the *Cerebellum* and the bakward Prominences.

Annu'et, a little Ring, which, in Heraldry, is a Mark of Diftinction which the fifth Brother of any Family ought to bear in his Coat of Arms. Alfo in Architecture, a narrow flat Moulding, ufed in the Bafes, Capitals, &c. of Columns.

Annull, (Lat.) to make void.

Annumerate, to put into the Number.

Annunciation, Delivery of a Meffage: Alfo *Lady-Day March* 25. fo call'd from the Angel's Meffage to *Mary*.

Anodynes, (Gr.) are fuch Remedies as alleviate or quite take away the Pain.

Anomalous, Unequal, Uneven, Irregular.

Anomaly, (in Grammar) an Irregularity in the Conjugations of Verbs or Declenfions of Nouns, when they do not follow the common Rule.

Ano-

A sample of etymologies dating from 1707 reveals how pervasive 'foreign' influences were in shaping the English language in many fields of knowledge, and suggests that the process of assimilating 'hard words' was conscious and deliberately cultivated. Blount, Thomas (1618–1679). Glossographia anglicana nova: or, A Dictionary, interpreting such hard words of whatever language, as are at present used in the English tongue, with their etymologies, definition, &c. Also the terms of divinity, law, physick, mathematicks, history, agriculture, logick, metaphysicks, grammar, poetry, musick, heraldry, architecture, painting, war, and all other arts and sciences are herein explain'd. London, 1707. https://catalog.hathitrust.org/Record/000115827 (University of Michigan catalog record) takes shape and gains prominence and usefulness from its interrelations with other natural languages; thus, the process that we commonly call translation is, at a deeper level, one of the processes that produces 'international' languages. In the long history of interrelations between natural languages there have been, since the invention of printing, two major transitions or breakthroughs that have altered and accelerated those interrelations by changing the communications media through which the natural languages made contact with each other. The first breakthrough was the transition from written and printed media to electric analog media such as audio recording technology, radio and television. The second transition, which is taking place today, at the beginning of the third millennium, is the transition from analog to electronic digital media, which now makes it possible for interrelations between natural languages to take place in real time.

The First Transition: Bridging Linguistic and Cultural Differences in Real Time

> *Interpreting is a form of Translation in which a first and final rendition in another language is produced on the basis of a one-time presentation of an utterance in a source language.* (Kade cited in Pöchhacker 2004: 11)

Although lay interpretation has existed from time immemorial, and although professional interpreters have been used for international negotiations at least since about 1600, when Latin fell out of use as a universal language, the art which we now call simultaneous interpretation or conference interpreting is of relatively recent vintage as disciplines go, dating roughly from the Nuremberg trials of 1945–1946,[54] a landmark proceeding during which a way had to be found to translate lengthy, complex arguments and witness statements in four languages in real time, since the thousands of hours and pages of testimony involved would otherwise have taken many years to translate, making the trials impossible. Archival film excerpts of interpreters in action at the International Military Tribunal may be seen at the following web page of the United States Holocaust Memorial Museum:

https://www.ushmm.org/wlc/en/media_fi.php?ModuleId=10007148&MediaId=5677

See also the film 'The Interpreters: A Historical Perspective' http://aiic.net/p/1410[55]

See also this video on multilingualism by Michael Møller, former Director General of the United Nations Office at Geneva:

https://www.youtube.com/watch?v=kxYXC_N8Ua4&feature=youtu.be

After Nuremberg, the earliest effort to recruit large numbers of simultaneous interpreters for the United Nations in 1947 was done by talent-scouting, a method still sometimes used today[56] in the form of competitive examinations held in different cities worldwide. The head of that operation, US Army Lieutenant Colonel Leon Dostert, described the requirements at the time as follows: 'Knowledge of language is only the basic requirement. [...] Our translators have to be alert mentally, they have to have a broad and fluent vocabulary, a good voice and some gift of oratory, and above all, they have to be able to understand what is being said even before they hear the end of the sentence.'[57] Having had the privilege to work for two decades with that first pioneering genera-tion of UN interpreters, the author can attest to the fact that those requirements stated in 1947 have remained true down to the present time, but others have been added, such as the ability to cope with speeches delivered at high speed. That increase in the average speed of delivery of speeches in turn has driven the development of techniques that interpreters must rely upon to deal with complexity and stress on a day-to-day basis.

Regular users of interpretation nowadays have become 'sophisticated consumers', routinely demanding a consistently high level of performance, while also recognizing the value of the service they demand. In a survey of over 200 users of interpretation services commissioned in 1993–1994 by the International Association of Conference Interpreters (AIIC) one of the most interesting findings was the following: 'Conference participants... realize that the broad educational and cultural background for which interpreters are envied does not come ready-made but has to be worked on continuously.'[58]

The same survey found that users were aware of the fact that interpre-tation is not a mere translation of the spoken word but is an act of cultural mediation, conveying the intellectual and emotional content of the origi-nal.[59] As noted by Robin Setton,[60] the interpreter's 'special skill is in ana-lyzing and storing very different incoming messages and repackaging them so that not only information, but also emphasis, and style if possible, are conveyed in the target language with its own words and syntax, and its own culturally specific ways of debating, informing, convincing, prais-ing or recommending.'[61] At the intergovernmental level, the formal requirements for interpreters now spelled out, for example, by the European Parliament reflect that high standard: 'To work at the European Parliament, training or experience as a conference interpreter are neces-sary. Interpreters should have a full university education and exception-ally good knowledge of languages. Versatility, analytical skills and complete mastery of the mother tongue are vital. Finally, the almost unlimited range of subjects covered in parliamentary debate requires extensive general knowledge and considerable expertise in all areas of European Union activity'.[62] These statements reveal a clear expectation among regular users of professional-level conference interpretation: they expect interpreters to have both the necessary cultural background and the necessary training in interpretation skills to convey the whole message. To that end, sound curricula and standards have now been formulated[63] and training programs leading to master-level credentials, e.g. the Masters in Conference Interpreting (MCI), have been created at several universities.[64]

Multilingual Dialogue

Important public debates and the conclusions of public bodies need to be followed and understood by as many people in the world as possible. Yet, that need has not always been recognized. At Nuremberg, legal and procedural principles combined with the political forces in play to require that the proceedings be held promptly in multiple languages. This was a daunting challenge and, once a technical solution had been devised, it was a matter of some surprise that such communication could be conducted successfully. At that time, an old conception of international relations which we might call the 'monolingual paradigm' held that communicating in a single language was more efficient, that the 'Babel' of multiple tongues was a source of confusion, and that translation (used here synonymously with interpretation) was a 'necessary evil' which international gatherings had to tolerate when it was not possible to use a lingua franca. A corollary of that paradigm was the idea that when translation was used something was always 'lost'. It can just as well be argued that when a target-language functional equivalent does not seem to be an exact fit for the source-language item, it is because something has been 'gained', namely the 'missing' piece of the conceptual puzzle for which the target language seems unable to provide a word or lexeme but which the mind of the target-language speaker can nevertheless perceive given the context (or the locution would not seem 'incomplete').

Indeed some literary purists and linguistic pundits have viewed translation as an inherently unreliable and somewhat disreputable occupation ('*traduttore traditore*'), a lesser form of authorship. Some formalistic authors have taken such an extreme view of untranslatability as to proclaim that 'translation is impossible.' It is no accident that this paradigm coincided historically with the heyday of consecutive interpretation. Given the tedium that international meetings had to endure thanks to that practice, in which every speech, good or bad, had to be listened to repeatedly, it is hardly surprising that some people took a dim view of multilingual communication and perhaps secretly yearned for a global empire where everyone would be obliged to speak a single dominant lingua franca. The simplicity of that solution can seem appealing but since no particular language is inherently better suited than others to serve as the world language, any choice made under the monolingual paradigm implies some degree of imposition on the speakers of many other languages, sowing seeds of misunderstanding, discord, resentment and strife, just as it can in the domestic arena, where mandatory monolingualism was a source of tension in the workplace and for that reason has come to be prohibited under US Equal Employment Opportunity Commission rules as a form of national-origin discrimination. (See also endnote 24, for an example of prohibition of machine translation as a means to comply with multilingualism.)

Fortunately, the dominance of the monolingual paradigm seems to have waned, although many ethnic tensions still persist throughout the world. The picture that has now emerged, which we might term the 'multilingual paradigm', recognizes that communication in more than one language is not reductive; it does not detract from or obscure the meaning of what is being said, but may even clarify it. This is not surprising if one considers that most speakers are not professional communicators and are simply trying to deliver a statement as best they can, whereas a trained interpreter is analyzing it and working with the message, identifying rhetorical structures and key ideas, and seeking to give each one the proper coloring and emphasis. An interpretation of a speech done by a professional interpreter is, in a sense, an additional fine-tuning of the speech. With the advent of simultaneous interpreting, interpretation no longer slows down the pace of proceedings. We know from experience that most of what we say is said best in our mother tongue. And what an audience hears is best understood in their respective mother tongues. Errors or omissions committed in the process by experienced interpreters are actually no more frequent than the errors or omissions committed by speakers; speeches delivered by experienced conference interpreters are generally as good as the originals; and under favorable conditions it can happen that the interpretation of a speech may actually improve on the original. When the interpreter is given the opportunity to meet and speak with the speaker before the speech, he may have the same 'insider' perspective on the message to be conveyed as a speechwriter and may be able to produce a more cogent and articulate version than a purely extemporaneous speech would have been.

When people meet to talk, there are, in addition to linguistic considerations, related issues of logistics, group psychology and group dynamics at play. When single-language communication is imposed on meeting participants and some are forced to speak in an acquired language, fluency and clarity falter and the time spent on the meeting grows longer as misunderstandings are clarified and self-conscious speakers grope for words or struggle to say what they mean. A good example is that of a Japanese company that decided to impose English as the sole mandatory language at its board meetings: 'Mikitani was ruthless: He simply announced that the whole company was switching its operational language. No negotiation. Japanese out, English in. Don't speak English? Tough. Deal with it. Take night classes. Soon after the switch he conducted a board meeting entirely in English, and each time a nervous executive in a navy-blue suit asked cautiously if he might explain something in Japanese, the answer was no: Say it in English, or don't say it. The board meeting took twice as long as a normal one.'[65]

The rigidity of the monolingual framework of communication also spells a loss of spontaneity: conceptual compromises and breakthroughs that sometimes happen in the course of a spontaneous conversation among fluent interlocutors in a relaxed setting may also be lost. Interlocutors at a loss for words may appear to be at a loss for ideas, causing embarrassment, increasing tension and making disagreements seem more intractable than they actually are. And it may happen that outcomes reached under imposed monolingualism did not represent genuine informed consent, leading over the long term to allegations of duress or resulting in unworkable agreements.

In international relations, a key advantage of multilingual dialogue is that the respect shown by addressing an interlocutor in that person's own language is conducive to successful diplomacy or negotiation. The value of interpreters in performing this function is generally acknowledged by experienced diplomats, such as Madeleine Albright: 'Interpreters play a vital but overlooked part in diplomacy. The best ones are able to translate not only words but also points of emphasis and tone, and are careful to ensure that idiomatic expressions are not misunderstood. I grew very fond of those who interpreted regularly for me and also of some of the foreign interpreters, whose voices I came to know intimately.'[66]

Multilingual communication is more than a mere courtesy; it is a way of saying 'I value your opinion and consider you important enough that I want to make sure you understand me' and of implying 'I am confident that my message can be well put in your language as well as in mine.' To the extent that the speaker himself is able to speak his interlocutor's language, the effect is clear and impressive. But even if the message is conveyed through an interpreter, what matters is that it is being put in the language best understood by the listener, which enhances clarity and inspires confidence. In negotiations, especially over contentious issues, clarity builds trust, and trust is what the parties need to find common ground. Having to grasp a difficult point in an unfamiliar language is not conducive to that degree of clarity and tends to inspire misunderstanding and mistrust regardless of how well-intentioned the parties may be. A leading study on negotiation succinctly drives this point home: 'Without communication, there is no negotiation.... When the parties speak different languages the chance for misinterpretation is compounded.'[67] However, when speaking the same language means imposing a foreign language on some of the participants, there is generally a loss of fluency and no overall gain in clarity. Moreover, the participants who are not using their native tongue are immediately placed at a disadvantage, whereas multilingual dialogue should serve as a psychological equalizer between participants, especially in discussions that are adversarial. A delegate at an international assembly who is speaking his own language just as he would at home does not feel that he is constrained in his freedom of speech, treading on shifting ground, making undue concessions or giving in to foreign pressures. And when all language versions are heard simultaneously, no one is unfairly disadvantaged in a debate by having to wait longer than others to hear the point of a speech or unfairly advantaged by gaining additional time to think during the second iteration of the message. Sovereign equality in the use of languages fosters orderly debate and helps to put all speakers on equal footing.

John Graham, United States representative to the UN. Photo used by permission of Mr. Graham.
'The United Nations (and every other organization that works in multiple languages) depends utterly on the quality of interpretations. At my time at the UN, I was constantly amazed at how expert the interpreters were, even when diplomats who should have known better were speaking too fast and using indigenous slang and humor. So my hat is off to the dedicated professional interpreters who did and are still doing the world a great service.'
John Graham
United States Mission to the United Nations, 1977–1980

How Does Multilingualism Enhance Global Communication?

- Multilingual communication strengthens international agreements by ensuring that they are based on genuine communication and a complete exchange of ideas or meeting of the minds among all concerned. Providing multiple channels, multilingual communication ensures a fuller exposition of ideas than would be the case with one channel, i.e. one language. When multilateral agreements are reached subject to certain nuances or reservations, negotiating multilingually and drafting the outcome document in multiple authentic versions may enable agreement to be reached among a wider spectrum of parties than would otherwise be the case.

Bilateral communication or bilingual communication with a limited number of participants can sometimes take place with consecutive interpretation. Skilled interpreters with the proper training can minimize the redundancy and tedium inherent in the fact that every speech must be given twice even though some of the listeners have already gotten the point while others do not understand the second iteration. But consecutive interpretation obviously becomes unworkable when three or more languages are being spoken, let alone six as in the UN or 24 as in the European Union. For multilingual communication to take place in real time requires simultaneous interpretation. If it is performed by trained professionals the result is better than asking speakers of various languages to communicate through a single so-called 'international' language in which they may have limited proficiency. Of the six major global conferences in which the author interpreted during the 20 years of his career from 1982 to 2002, none could have taken place without simultaneous interpretation, since covering the languages of the 190+ participants in such global conferences implied using all six of the UN official languages[68] and sometimes a few more. (The rule at such conferences is that the representative of a state may use one of the six UN languages <u>or</u> his own national language, provided his statement is conveyed through his own interpreter into one of the UN languages. Moreover, interpretation in some language combinations may require the use of relay.) The issues addressed by those conferences were, by their nature, issues requiring consensus-based global solutions, since every country in the world was potentially affected by them and had a stake in the outcome; thus, no one could be left out by communication barriers lest any outcomes arrived at prove unworkable or subject to challenge. Each of these conferences arrived at an outcome that represented a step forward, however imperfect, in resolving the issues it had addressed, and that progress could not have been achieved but for the possibility of exhaustively discussing issues in depth using languages that all the delegates could understand. Striving for universality also encourages states to be engaged and compliant because they will see the undertaking as more likely to succeed, since the strength of international law is commensurate with the breadth of the consensus supporting it.

Major global diplomatic conferences using six languages (Arabic, Chinese, English, French, Russian, Spanish) from 1982 to 2002

Third United Nations Conference on the Law of the Sea; Jamaica, December 1982: Session adopting the United Nations Convention on the Law of the Sea. The 1982 UN Convention on the Law of the Sea (UNCLOS), which entered into force in 1994, is the product of 14 years of work by over 160 countries representing all regions and legal systems and has been ratified by 166 countries.[69] The most comprehensive multilateral treaty in the history of public international law, the Convention's 320 articles and nine annexes cover all uses of the oceans and their resources, governing two thirds of the earth's surface.

United Nations Security Council: first summit meeting of heads of state of Security Council member states; New York City, 31 January, 1992: At its first Summit meeting on 31 January 1992 the Council discussed its wide responsibility for the maintenance of peace and security. Presidential statement S/23500 following the summit noted the changed environment following the end of the Cold War and stressed the importance of strengthening and increasing the effectiveness of the UN.

United Nations Conference on Environment & Development (Earth Summit) Rio de Janeiro, June 1992, laid the foundations for the environmental revolution and for conventions such as the Climate Change Convention, the Kyoto Protocol, the Convention on Biological Diversity, and the Paris Agreement of 2015. Hundreds of thousands of people from all walks of life were drawn into the Rio process. They persuaded their leaders to go to Rio and join other nations in making the difficult decisions needed to ensure a healthy planet for generations to come.

The summit's message – that nothing less than a transformation of our attitudes and behaviour would bring about the necessary changes – was transmitted by almost 10,000 on-site journalists and heard by millions around the world.

United Nations General Assembly; Special Commemorative Meeting at the head of government level, marking the Fiftieth Anniversary of the United Nations; New York City, October 1995.

United Nations Diplomatic Conference of Plenipotentiaries on the Establishment of an International Criminal Court; Rome, 15

June–17 July 1998. On 17 July 1998, the Conference adopted the Rome Statute of the International Criminal Court, which was opened for signature on 17 July 1998. The International Criminal Court has since been established to bring to trial the perpetrators of the most serious crimes of concern to the international community as a whole, i.e. the crime of genocide, crimes against humanity, war crimes, and the crime of aggression.

International Conference on Financing for Development; Monterrey, Mexico, 18–22 March 2002. This first United Nations-hosted conference to address key financial and development issues attracted 50 Heads of State or Government, over 200 ministers as well as leaders from the private sector and civil society, and senior officials of all the major intergovernmental financial, trade, economic, and monetary organizations. Their statements to the plenaries (in text and in video) and the Monterrey Consensus provide a picture of the new global approach to financing development. The Monterrey Conference also marked the first quadripartite exchange of views between governments, civil society, the business community, and the institutional stakeholders on global economic issues. These global discussions involved over 800 participants in twelve separate roundtables.

- Multilingual communication enhances the quality of communications and the richness of a language by bringing into the picture more culturally diverse sources and references, e.g. figures of speech, proverbs, concepts and values peculiar to a given culture or aptly codified in its language. For example, the proverbial maxim 'Conquête trop aisée est bientôt méprisée' finds its way into French from Shakespeare ('Too light winning makes the prize light.'). Or, taking an example from the realm of political terminology, both key terms in the phrase 'the *junta* staged a *coup*' are borrowings from other languages (Spanish and French) that are have become anglicized and are commonly used in English because these 'foreign' words evocatively point to their referents.
- Multilingual communication encourages spontaneity of discourse and hence originality of thinking. Most speakers, however fluent they may be in a second language, will prepare and write out in advance a speech they know they must deliver in that language. They will then read out the speech in a style of delivery that will often be rushed, monotonous, labored, uninspiring or pedantic in style. They will be less prone to those failings if they can speak in their own language. Speaking one's own language makes it easier to be frank, sincere, or sensitive. One can also be more precise in expressing one's feelings and less afraid of saying the wrong thing.

- Multilingual communication fosters accuracy. We know from experience that, whatever language we may be using, in whatever context, we tend immediately to revert to our native tongue when we have something important or complicated to say, because we are more confident of getting it right. In conference interpretation systems such as those of the UN and the EU, where interpreters work into their native languages, accuracy is better served.
- Multilingual communication helps to minimize miscommunication and misconceptions resulting from speakers' limited language fluency and their limited knowledge of the source language(s) or of the 'international language' of the day. Since the degree of fluency needed for public speaking is high, a significant proportion of foreign-service personnel lack such fluency in the language(s) required to perform public representation duties to which they are assigned. For instance, in the United States, a report by the Office of the Inspector General found that there is '...an actual skills gap, where the officer lacks any host-country language training or has insufficient language training for the public diplomacy job. For example, the information officer at Embassy Santo Domingo needed language training to work in Spanish with the local press. In Saudi Arabia, none of the public diplomacy officers had received the Arabic language training required for their positions. At Embassy Budapest, most of the officers were capable and ready to carry out public diplomacy outreach, but the difficulty of the Hungarian language limited the number of officers who could make a presentation in Hungarian. Previous work by the Advisory Group on Public Diplomacy and GAO has drawn attention to the language skills gap as a critical challenge that is not limited to public diplomacy. A recent GAO report said that 35 percent of Department staff in public diplomacy positions did not meet language requirements. Some of the officers GAO met with had the language proficiency required for their assignments but nevertheless said they were not sufficiently fluent to effectively perform their jobs.'[70]

A good example of the everyday limits of most people's fluency is the word 'liberal', which can carry very different and even opposite meanings depending on the context in English, French and Spanish, and is frequently misused by speakers of all three languages.[71] An experienced interpreter will have been prepared, as part of his/her terminology training, to find appropriate wording or phraseology to deal with the intended meanings.

- Multilingual communication helps to ensure that messages or opinions that are strongly held get across to those that matter. Where ethnically and linguistically diverse groups of stakeholders involved in an issue are empowered to use their own languages, they will speak more freely and they tend to be listened to because their arguments will be better expressed and therefore more cogent and persuasive. In this way, multilingual communication helps to foster respect for human rights and democratic outcomes.

- In a controversy or dispute, multilingual communication can sometimes help to break the deadlock of entrenched positions by introducing novel perspectives or ideas and opening up additional avenues for seeking solutions, e.g. the dramatic effect that adoption of the concept of *transparency* (*glasnost*) had on Soviet political discourse.[72]

- Multilingual communication fosters trust. In diplomatic conferences, confidence in the integrity of the communication process, i.e. the interpreters, is essential. A conference participant whose language is not included among those in use at a conference may suspect that he is being left out of the action or that deals are being made behind his back. Underlying tensions which may exist between country representatives can worsen if the interpreters available do not inspire trust. In certain cases of great tension, delegates may prefer to speak in or translate into a language they do not thoroughly master rather than pass through an interpreter who is seen as unreliable. This is why it is important to ensure that the interpreters chosen are of the necessary caliber and have experience in dealing with situations where tact and savoir-faire are needed.[73]

- Multilingual communication helps to make possible selection of spokesmen and negotiators according to their substantive expertise rather than their knowledge of an acquired language. When interpretation is available, it is not necessary to take language knowledge into account in deciding who will attend a meeting and act as spokesman or representative; consequently, it is easier to select delegates solely on the basis of their qualifications and abilities. In this way, multilingual communication supports useful specialization among meeting participants and enhances the quality of the discussion.

- Similarly, multilingualism enhances transparency and accountability by making it possible for the general public and the body politic to monitor and understand what a nation's diplomatic representatives say in international fora and how well they say it. In this regard, see the comments of the Vice President of the European Parliament, Miguel Angel Martínez Martínez, in the following video (at 7:46).

  https://www.youtube.com/watch?v=_lOInrJ5YGE

- The interpreter sometimes serves as cultural broker, adapting or clarifying human values, cultural features and spoken nuances that may not be readily understandable in a simple translation or may not have the same connotations in the source and target languages. For example, in a conversation between Presidents Gorbachev and Reagan about Red Square, it had to be explained to the latter that the Russian language uses the same word (*krasnaya*) for the concepts 'red' and 'beautiful'.[74]

- Interpretation can on occasion serve as a buffer in an adversarial discussion, making it possible to use the interpreter as a conduit for certain ideas and positions. It is sometimes possible to say things through a linguistic intermediary that one would be reluctant to say directly in one's own language or using the language of an adversary.[75] Interpreters often permit diplomatic 'feelers' to be extended or negotiating 'trial balloons' to be floated.

- Multilingual communication supports nuanced expression of meaning, often paving the way for compromise solutions. In diplomacy, where the value of a word carries weight, it is particularly important to pay attention to idiom and nuances. Idiom and nuance are more easily and effectively expressed and understood in a native language that one speaks spontaneously and fluently than in an acquired language or a compromise lingua franca such as 'international English' in which idioms tend to give way to clichés and nuances tend to be eclipsed by bureaucratic boilerplate that is often affected by poor verbatim translations and which strips English of its admirable brevity and expressiveness. For example, here is a sentence from a speech at the UN by former President Nestor Kirchner of Argentina.

  > A large part of the problem lies, perhaps, in the lack of correspondence between declarations – true expressions of wish – and acts.

  > Much of the problem may lie in the mismatch between words, however truly felt, and deeds.

  The first version is typical 'official Spanglish': English influenced by formal Spanish lexicon and syntax. It is what actually appeared in print in the English translation of the speech that was circulated by the Argentine delegation when President Kirchner gave the speech. It is 21 words long. The second version is a restatement of the same idea in normal, idiomatic contemporary English. It is only 16 words long, yet is much clearer and more incisive. And, naturally, the shorter, idiomatic version is more suited to simultaneous interpretation, especially bearing in mind that some parts of this speech were delivered at the rate of 170 words per minute. (See Chapter 2 in this volume.)

- Multilingualism also lends vigor to cultural diplomacy. States often undertake some form of cultural diplomacy to improve their image abroad and to further their foreign policy aims, and speaking the language of the listener can be a valuable means of expressing and earning respect. Thus, former President John F. Kennedy undertook the task of mastering French with a view to conducting negotiations with President Charles De Gaulle, and, according to a 2012 interview with the Council of Foreign Relations, former President Jimmy Carter, who studied Spanish at the US Naval Academy, would often speak Spanish at conferences in Latin American countries, although in situations where nuances mattered, he insisted on the use of professional inter-preters. Obviously, statesmen of the stature of Kennedy and Carter could have allowed themselves to speak English wherever they went, but they chose not to, and the reason has perhaps been best expressed by another great statesman, Nelson Mandela: 'If you talk to a man in a language he understands, that goes to his head. If you talk to him in his language, that goes to his heart.' We were treated to a good exam-ple of this when Secretary of State John Kerry spoke French, German and Italian during his first European tour and offered some brief remarks in very good French at a joint news conference in Paris with French Foreign Minister Laurent Fabius.

http://www.youtube.com/watch?v=YVcI50YBnLg&feature=plcp&list=FLUouxpVj7RCUfyYntvXW1Vg (at 4.50–6.00)

Similarly, during a meeting between US President Barack Obama and Indian Prime Minister Narendra Modi aimed at elevating the two leaders' 'strategic partnership', President Obama took the initiative to set the right tone by greeting Prime Minister Modi in his own lan-guage, saying 'Kem cho, Mr. Prime Minister'.[76]

Because of the advantages summarized above, conducting multilateral diplomatic and economic relations in the multilingual mode has become the standard way to conduct world affairs. Conference interpreting has come into its own as a profession and the world has come to rely on conference interpretation for cross-cultural communication in real time. Whether in international organizations or in national deliberative and legislative bodies, language barriers are no longer a major obstacle and urgent discussions on pressing issues can take place without delay. But there has been a parallel development: the rate at which speeches are delivered at international meetings has increased steadily, for sev-eral reasons. There are now 196 independent countries in the world and among the 7000 languages spoken today[77] the number of languages being used as a medium of international communication is growing in parallel with recognition of people's right to use their native languages. The European Union, for example, now uses 24 languages. Consequently, there are a growing number of interlocutors on the world scene speaking a growing number of different languages and making their statements in the expectation of being immediately understood. And they all have a great deal to say about a growing number of press-ing issues. But for practical and logistical reasons there are still only about 12 hours in the day that can be used as conference time and those hours must be equitably shared among the many speakers vying for the rostrum and the microphone. The result is that spokespersons resort to speaking faster and faster during their all-too-brief turn on the world stage, further complicating the interpreter's task.

The Legislative Mandate for Intergovernmental Interpreting

In organizing language services, training linguistic practitioners or setting standards, it is important to be mindful of the different legislative rationales for domestic and international interpretation services. Within a given country, a person's inability to speak the majority national language proficiently may be treated as a handicap that needs to be overcome by accommodations or remedial legislation that will give that disadvantaged person equal access to courts or social services. The premise of remedial legislation is that there is something wrong that needs to be rectified. If a person is denied a right because of his/her gender or color, for example, it is well established that this is a denial of equal rights or of equal protection under the law, since the individual cannot be held responsible for the kind of physical or biological feature on which the denial is based. However, where language rights are concerned, the characteristic in question, although innate, may not automatically entitle the person to enforceable equal protection under the law, because it is sometimes theoretically possible for a speaker of a minority language to learn the majority language. Consequently, the minority language speaker seeking equal rights is sometimes made to carry the additional burden of proving that there is an explicit legislative mandate requiring him/her to be granted equal language rights, and such a specific mandate cannot always be found. For instance, in the Canadian Supreme Court decision of 20 November 2015 in the case of *R v Caron & Boulet*, the court denied the francophone litigants' appeal because there was no specific enactment on record in their province requiring laws to be published in French as well as in English.[78] Decisions like this one represent something close to a presumption that, by default, everyone speaks the majority language from birth, or should be expected to learn it, unless there is proof to the contrary formally embodied in a legal enactment.

In the United States domestic context, court interpreting is mandated by principles of due process and by statutory provisions such as Title VI of the Civil Rights Act of 1964, Executive Order 13166 and the US Federal Court Interpreters Act of 1978. In other words, the mandate for provision of interpretation in the legal arena grows out of an acknowledged situation of de facto inequality, in which some people are disadvantaged by their lack of proficiency in the dominant language. Interpretation practices in other public service and community settings tend to follow the standard set by court systems.

In international relations, however, there is in principle no dominant language. On the contrary, any implication of dominance or inequality is avoided because there is an implicit recognition of the fact that, when it comes to choice of languages, 'the medium is the message', i.e. the choice of the language used to convey a message or to frame a debate itself carries a message. In relations between sovereign states the choice of language(s) for everyday communication is guided largely by practical considerations, while the choice of language(s) for higher-level diplomatic functions or multilateral negotiations is influenced by considerations of national identity and prestige and tends to be viewed as an attribute of sovereignty.[79] A French or Spanish diplomat may be content to exchange technical information with other countries in English if that is the most practical means available but one will not find him making a formal policy address before the North Atlantic Council or the UN General Assembly in English even if he is completely fluent in the language. It is by speaking his native tongue that he best fulfils his responsibility to make himself clearly and fully understood. A major address by a national figure nowadays is usually translated by a variety of sources, official and non-governmental, and rendered in a variety of versions, some better than others, in the home language and in other languages. Also, an important aspect of any country's foreign policy is making its national culture and language known and respected in the world at large.[80]

Naturally, observing these principles in practice implies substantial institutional arrangements. How are such large-scale language services managed?[81] One assumption thus far has been that the services must be primarily in-house. The view at the European Union, for example, is that 'An internal service is essential if suitable interpreting is always to be available at short notice and if overall quality and confidentiality are to be guaranteed'.[82] This assumption generally holds true and tends to ensure that there will continue to be a substantial number of full-time positions for intergovernmental interpreters, even though under current conditions the optimal mix between staff and free-lance interpreters is viewed as being about 50/50. The European Union's CIRCABC website is a good example of a platform that enables large volumes of translation to be done offsite by external contractors who are given access to institutional resources, such as terminology, by means of the online platform.[83]

A second basic assumption has thus far been that an organization's official languages will be treated equally, i.e. given fully symmetrical coverage. In the UN, the governing legislative mandates make clear that operating in the multilingual mode is done not only for practicality or convenience but as of right.[84] In 1995, General Assembly Resolution 50/11 on Multilingualism declared that '…the universality of the United Nations *and its corollary, multilingualism*, entail for each State Member of the Organization, irrespective of the official language in which it expresses itself, *the right and the duty to make itself understood and to understand others*…'.[85] In 1999 this was followed by a Report of the Secretary General providing for detailed measures to implement multilingualism within the UN Secretariat.[86] In 2000, a further General Assembly resolution provided for the appointment of a senior official as coordinator of questions relating to multilingualism throughout the Secretariat.[87] In 2001, a more comprehensive report of the Secretary General analyzed several issues involved in implementing the principle of equal treatment of languages while making the best use of available resources.[88]

In addition to the growing volume of communications and the growing number of languages used by the EU, a further noteworthy development is the growing diversity of languages used in international courts and tribunals, including some heretofore rarely heard in international fora. For example, the International Criminal Tribunal for the Former Yugoslavia now employs linguists with Serbian and Croatian in their language combination, and the first case tried before the International Tribunal for the Law of the Sea when the author served there as Head of Linguistic Services included simultaneous interpretation of witness testimony in Wolof.[89]

Thus, it seems that intergovernmental organizations have come to appreciate the full import of the right to multilingualism as a corollary of 'the right and duty to make oneself understood and to understand others': it resides in the fact that although all languages are of comparable usefulness as tools of communication[90] any message is best expressed in the language of the speaker and best understood in the language of the listener.

Against this background of steady growth in the volume of communication and the number of languages in use as conference languages, it became apparent early on that intergovernmental organizations stood to gain a great deal from coordinating their efforts at defining the contours of the language professions, setting consistent standards and pursuing joint training initiatives. In July 2001 in Geneva, an open-ended Working Group on training was set up with the mandate of reporting to IAMLADP[91] in Vienna in 2002 on training of language staff in five key areas: translation, conference interpretation, editing, précis-writing and proof-reading. Input was received from international organizations, members of IAMLADP and universities. The Working Group completed its mandate and reported to IAMLADP in 2002. A number of points emerged from the findings, such as the shortage of qualified staff, the need for continuing education, the lack of recognition of linguists' role and work, the gap between employers' needs and university training and the need to adapt to new technologies in the workplace.[92] These and other similar issues have continued to be discussed in the framework of IAMLADP in a series of subsequent meetings.[93]

The Organization of Intergovernmental Interpreting

Bilateral contacts

In bilateral contacts, intergovernmental or diplomatic interpreting is generally arranged by the respective foreign services involved. Both in-person and remote modes are widely used. In bilateral talks there may be a particular individual interpreter who is recognized or preferred as being expert in certain language combinations and/or subjects and who accompanies the foreign minister or envoy on assignments in which that expertise is called for. The dynamics of a bilateral encounter are such that a failure to communicate may create an 'awkward silence' that may be experienced as an embarrassment or may become an obstacle to further negotiations. For example, according to Philippine news reports of 24 November 2015, there had been a perceived 'snub' or 'aloofness' during the meeting between President Aquino and President Xi Jinping on their way to the APEC Business Advisory Council; however, President Aquino rectified those reports, explaining that during that situation they had simply been unable to talk because of the lack of an interpreter.[94]

Paradoxically, although an interpreter may be most noticed in his absence, his presence must always be discreet and unobtrusive. The interpreter must also be bound by strict secrecy so that the principals feel free to express themselves and communicate confidential information to each other without fear of 'leaks' or embarrassing public disclosures. This means, among other things, that they cannot be required to reveal or give testimony about the conversations they interpret, as illustrated by the public statement below issued by the International Association of Conference Interpreters.

Statement by the Executive Committee of AIIC, 19 July 2018

The International Association of Conference Interpreters (AIIC), in reaction to the suggestion that the interpreter present at the recent meeting between President Trump and President Putin may be required to give testimony, wishes to recall the principle enshrined in Article 2a of AIIC's Code of Professional Ethics:

AIIC Code of Professional Ethics

Art. 2 a) Members of the Association shall be bound by the strictest secrecy, which must be observed towards all persons and with regards to all information disclosed in the course of the practice of the profession at any gathering not open to the public.

If statesmen are to speak freely, they must be able to trust interpreters unreservedly not to reveal confidential information. Hence the importance of upholding the cardinal principle applied worldwide since WWII, that interpreters should never be obliged to give testimony.

Signed, 19 July 2018

It is a long-standing convention in formal diplomatic interpreting that each side brings its own interpreter, usually of its own nationality. This arrangement has several advantages:

- confidence and confidentiality: each side feels it can trust its interpreter to work in its best interest and not divulge confidential information;

- each interpreter can monitor the translation done by the other interpreter and warn of any discrepancies;
- the division of work between two interpreters provides some relief if the meeting is prolonged.

When a government spokesman must speak in a multilateral gathering where his language is not provided for, he must bring along his own interpreter, or arrange for what is known as a 'pointer' – a delegation member who sits with the interpreters in the booth, listens to the speech, and runs his finger line by line down a printed translation of the speech to enable one of the interpreters to read out the translation while keeping pace with the speaker.

Multilateral contacts

In multilateral fora, interpretation is organized by the secretariats of international organizations concerned and the requirements differ from one organization to another, although there are some common features. The interpreter is not normally expected to be of the same nationality as the speaker but must satisfy a number of criteria and must have passed examinations.

What follows is a description adapted from the website of the interpretation service of the United Nations Office at Geneva (UNOG), where the author worked for several years.[95] This service is part of the Department for General Assembly and Conference Management, Meetings and Publishing Division, encompassing the interpretation services of both Geneva and New York, of which the author served as Deputy Director. The UNOG interpretation service provides a good microcosm of how large-scale interpretation services operate. The Service comprises six language sections providing simultaneous interpretation is in the official languages of the Organization to an average of 2700 meetings of United Nations Conferences and bodies per year at Geneva Headquarters and in the field.

The Service is staffed by a total of 80 conference interpreters, whose job is defined as follows: **A conference interpreter is a professional language and communication expert who works in multilingual meetings and renders a message from one language into another, naturally and fluently, adopting the delivery, tone and convictions of the speaker.** The work of a conference interpreter is an oral intellectual exercise which is quite distinct from written translation and requires different training and qualifications. **Interpreters' work is subject to constant, immediate and very public scrutiny; no supervisory review or revision is possible before their 'product' is delivered.**

The ability to interpret is a skill many claim but few truly possess. Consider the process of simultaneous interpretation: interpreters listen to the speaker, understand the message and convert it into another language, speak to the delegates, monitor their output to ensure accurate and elegant delivery, all the while absorbing the next part of the speech. Consequently, they must exercise great concentration while working under constant pressure in order to maintain a high standard of split-second accuracy and be must be able to assimilate a broad range of subjects and specialized terminology. The following table is an approximate representation of the factors involved in the interpreting process.

THE INTERPRETING PROCESS

LISTENING	
COMPREHENSION / RECEPTIVITY / EMPATHY	MEMORIZING
PROCESSING	THINKING
ANALYSIS / VISUALIZATION/ REFORMULATION / MIMESIS / INFERENCE / EXTRAPOLATION / DEDUCTION	
SPEAKING / EXPRESSION	REMEMBERING
REPRODUCTION OF MEANING ARTICULATION, ENUNCIATION MEANING & EMOTION MODULATED BY TONE, INTONATION	

How interpreters work at the United Nations

Conference interpretation can be performed in three ways: simultaneously, consecutively and by whispering (*chuchotage*).[96] In simultaneous mode, the interpreters sit in sound-proof booths where the speaker is heard through headphones and they deliver a running interpretation transmitted through a microphone to participants in the meeting who wear earphones. The consecutive mode consists of the interpreter sitting at the conference table, taking notes and re-delivering the statement in another language. Situations arise in which it is impractical to provide simultaneous interpretation equipment, e.g. urgent meetings held on short notice, impromptu interviews, confidential one-on-one negotiations, press conferences held outdoors or on an airport tarmac, confidential medical or psychiatric evaluations, interrogations, etc. For such encounters, consecutive interpretation remains the norm. It is thought by some that the use of a single interpreter rather than a team increases confidentiality, since there are no electronic or digital connections to be tapped or hacked. Consecutive is also used by court systems at trials and hearings, and by lawyers for depositions. It has the further advantage of providing brief pauses during which the participants can think about what has been said and formulate their next question or statement. Performing consecutive interpretation, whether in training or on the job, also helps interpreters to develop skills that are useful for simultaneous interpretation.

Whispering (*chuchotage*), also occasionally used in certain working environments such as field missions, press conferences and high-level bilateral private meetings, consists of the interpreter simultaneously whispering the interpretation directly to a very limited audience, with or without mobile equipment.

The United Nations relies mainly on simultaneous interpretation because its work often involves large multiple-language meetings.[97] The organization has six official languages: Arabic (A), Chinese (C), English (E), French (F), Russian (R), Spanish (S) and two working languages: English and French. All United Nations staff are required to possess at least one of the working languages. Conferences and meetings of United Nations bodies may be conducted in as many as all six official languages. Consequently there are six corresponding language sections ('booths') in the Interpretation Service. Normally, only these languages will be used at United Nations meetings. If a Member State wishes to use a non-United Nations language, it must make the necessary arrangements for that language to be interpreted into one of the official languages.

Interpreters are identified by the language they work into, which at the United Nations is always their mother tongue in the E, F, R and S booths. Thus an English (booth) interpreter interprets from other official languages into English. English is that interpreter's 'active' or 'target' language, while the two or more other languages from which he/she interprets are referred to as 'passive,' or 'source' languages. Because certain language combinations at the level required for UN interpreting work are very rare, this structure is not applied to the Arabic and Chinese booths, where interpreters work both into and from their mother tongues. This dispenses E, F, R, S interpreters from having to interpret from Arabic and Chinese directly. Instead, they relay from Arabic or Chinese interpreters who are interpreting into English or French. Consequently, as the A and C booths work non-stop, they are staffed with three interpreters per booth while the E, F, R and S booths are staffed with two per booth.

Challenges Facing Intergovernmental Conference Interpretation

As the requirements of the profession evolve, today's challenge is one of finding and preparing qualified professionals, and solutions must focus on education and training, as well as on devising methods of testing and recruitment which ensure that qualitative standards are not eroded in the attempt to cope with the quantitative surge.[98] In dealing with that challenge, there are two hurdles emerging that can be dubbed the 'cybernetic siren-song' and the 'pedagogical pitfall'. The cybernetic siren-song is the temptation to believe that the availability of artificial intelligence, computerized word processing or computer-assisted translation programs will make it unnecessary for humans to invest the time and effort needed to master natural languages (native or foreign) and become conversant with their cultures, a view which one hopes no serious researcher in computational linguistics would subscribe to and which surely amounts to a kind of wishful thinking. The pedagogical pitfall is the tendency to believe that by describing a complex mental process to a student, or requiring the student to write a paper about it or be tested on it, one has taught him/her how to perform it. The only antidote these two fallacies is to stoically accept the truisms 'No pain, no gain' and 'Practice makes perfect'. Developments in communications technology will generally not make interpreting easier to practice but they have the potential to vastly extend its scope and relevance.

The Second Transition: Bridging Linguistic, Cultural and Geographical Distances in Real Time – The Promise of Remote Interpreting Through Advances in Videoconferencing

Simultaneous interpretation made it possible for international relations to take place multilingually in real time, meeting the language needs of the many international fora and conferences that developed during the 20th century thanks to the ability of modern transportation to bring together large numbers of diplomats, officials and experts from many countries in one place to discuss specific issues at appropriate venues. Today, the speed of simultaneous interpretation combined with the speed and high fidelity of digital audio and video communications are making it possible to conduct virtual multilingual dialogues in real time over great distances among people in different places, reducing the need for people to travel in order to confer with each other. Remote interpreting can also be used to give a multilingual dimension to a gathering with mass attendance, such as the 2018 World Youth Day in Panama, where events were broadcast in five languages from a central simultaneous interpreting facility to some 100,000 attendees at locations around the city. Some of the possible modalities of distance interpreting given current technologies were recently outlined by AIIC interpreter Andrew Constable:

Also of interest is a recent review of developments in remote interpreting technologies by Tatiana Kaplun, which points to the possibilities that are being opened up in this new world and the adaptations that interpreters will need to devise: Tatiana Kaplun. 'A fresh look at remote simultaneous interpreting'. aiic.net December 21, 2018. http://aiic.net/p/8725

A striking example of successful distance interpreting took place at the 2012 World Economic Forum, where the Prime Minister of Japan, speaking Japanese ten thousand kilometers away in Tokyo was brought into a

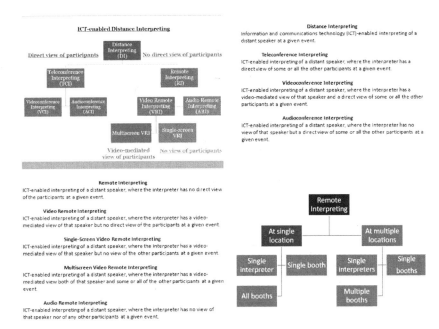

From a presentation by Andrew Constable, interpreter for the International Criminal Court, at Rimini meeting of AIIC, 2015. Reproduced by permission.

conversation taking place in English in Davos, Switzerland. Due to the size of the onstage monitor used, the 'remote' participant was actually the most visible presence in the conference hall. It was also noteworthy that, despite the vast geographical and linguistic obstacles that were being successfully bridged, the expectation of the participants and the audience was that the system should work seamlessly, and a momentary technical delay that occurred as the remote signal was being brought in became a source of mild embarrassment and amusement to the participants. What technology makes possible sooner or later becomes real, and we are increasingly seeing multilingual real-time virtual conferences[99] being routinely convened in cyberspace using simultaneous interpretation and videoconferencing, with speakers and interpreters participating from different locations.[100] The following examples in which the author participated show how this technology evolved over a period of about 30 years.

(1)   New York City, November 1980: I provided simultaneous interpretation of exchanges by a panel of commentators during live news coverage of the 1980 US presidential election by a French television network. The program was being transmitted by satellite to France.

(2)   New York City, 24 August 1994: I provided simultaneous interpretation tor news coverage by a US television network of a press conference given in Havana by Cuban President Fidel Castro concerning migration issues. The signal was being received from Havana.

(3)   New York City, 9 June 1994: I provided simultaneous interpretation during a teleconference concerning the White Helmets deployment in Haiti. The participants were UN Secretary General Boutros Boutros Ghali, OAS Secretary General Cesar Gaviria Trujillo, President Juan Carlos Wasmosy of Paraguay, President Carlos Saul Menem of Argentina and President Gonzalo Sanchez de Losada of Bolivia. Secretary General Boutros Ghali was in the studio in New York, the three presidents were in South America, and Secretary General Gaviria was in Washington. The connection to Washington was by telephone line, and the connection to South America was by satellite, routed through Madrid.

(4)   New York City, 26 October 1995: I provided simultaneous interpretation for live news coverage of an interview on economic issues with President Jacques Chirac. The signal was being received by satellite from Paris.

(5)   New York City, December 1995: I provided simultaneous interpretation of live news coverage of an address by French Prime Minister Alain Juppé to the National Assembly. The signal was being received by satellite from Paris.

(6)   New York City, December 1995: I provided simultaneous interpretation of live news coverage of a press conference given by President Jacques Chirac and Chancellor Helmut Kohl. The signal was being received by satellite from Baden-Baden, Germany.

(7)   New York City, 16 May 1996: I provided interpretation at a teleconference concerning economic development issues between members of the Parliament of Argentina in Buenos Aires and two UN officials (Mr. Joly and Mr. Zumbado) in New York. The signal was being received by satellite from Argentina.

(8)   New York City, 16 September 1996: I provided simultaneous interpretation at a meeting of the UN Administrative Committee on Coordination dealing primarily with the Efficiency Board. The meeting was the first time that UN offices in New York, Geneva and Vienna had been linked for a joint session in real time via satellite. During the meeting, Under-Secretary General Joseph Connor observed, 'Now, Conference Services is experimenting with remote interpretation, more challenging technically, but with tremendous potential. I should tell you that you are participating in a test of another efficiency project today, an experiment in remote interpretation. My voice in New York is being interpreted in Geneva and Vienna. In the future, we won't have to be in the same room or even in the same time zone as our highly skilled interpreters. This too is a first for the UN.'

(9)   New York City, 19 April 2005 ABC Television network. Remote interpretation of live news coverage of the Papal Conclave and election of Pope Benedict XVI taking place in Rome.

(10) Michelin Corp., Greenville, South Carolina, 12-14 March 2013: I provided simultaneous interpretation at a multi-site technical seminar on tire production, with speakers participating in simultaneous seminars at Michelin headquarters in France, Brazil and Thailand.

In each of the situations described above, the speaker(s) being interpreted and/or the target audience hearing the interpretation were in different locations and, in some cases, in different time zones. It should be noted that when a conference spans two major cities it becomes possible for the conference organizers recruiting interpreters to draw on a larger and more diverse pool of qualified 'local' talent, which may result in savings on travel and lodging costs for the sponsor and may permit coverage of certain language combinations to be more easily achieved.

Having begun with a historical perspective, let me conclude this chapter by recalling a moment of crisis in our history that I witnessed as an interpreter, and end by venturing a historical prediction. I believe that in years to come the heightened security concerns that were ushered in by the attacks of 11 September 2001 will probably remain at the 'orange alert' state or higher, to use the terminology now in use at airports. That feeling has been with me since the morning of 12 September 2001, when I was one of the two English interpreters called in to New York City to service the emergency meeting of the UN Security Council which met that morning in response to the attack. Making my way through a deserted city where the dust was still falling from the destruction of the twin towers, I could not help wondering if the attacks were really over but I knew that despite the danger in the air the Security Council had to meet. I sensed that, for interpreters as for everyone else, things would never be the same again and security would become a constant concern. Today, one possible response to that concern would be remote interpreting, which has the potential to address not only the obstacle of physical distance but also some security situations where high-level gatherings could become targets of terrorism. Moreover, where a meeting must be arranged on short notice or when a problem of very 'rare' language combinations arises, remote interpreting can make it possible to find and use the best-qualified interpreters for the job even if they are remotely located and cannot be brought in time to the meeting venue. While bearing in mind that the interpreter's presence at the meeting venue is the best practice because it enables the interpreter to interact with the participants and be better informed, I believe that the possibilities offered by remote interpretation should also be explored.

2 Analyzing a Speech[101]

Interpreting a speech requires analysis of its content and structure. The interpreter analyzes the speech as (s)he hears it both to understand the message and to rearrange the contents as necessary in order to satisfy grammar and usage and to keep pace with the speaker while fitting the interpretation within the allocated time. At the phrasal level certain rearrangements are necessary because of rigid grammatical rules. For example, the normal sequence of adjectives in different languages dictates that they be given in a specific order: the French phrase 'petit chien blanc' must be rendered as 'small white dog', not 'small dog white'. At the sentence level, it is often possible to shift the sequence of phrases and clauses, e.g. to change the position of a general adverbial clause within a sentence in a way that makes the sentence clearer and shorter in English: 'Given the urgency of the problem, my government spares no effort in addressing it' > 'My government spares no effort in addressing the problem, given its urgency.' And at the level of the speech, it is sometimes possible to insert towards the end of the speech an idea or reference that the interpreter omitted or glossed over earlier due to pressure.

Interpreters nowadays work under increased pressure due to the trend towards an intensified and accelerated international and multicultural dialogue: representatives of more and more countries are speaking in more and more languages about more and more issues, with spokespersons having to speak ever faster because the need to accommodate so many speakers imposes time-limits on each one. It is a fact of life today that while practical, logistical and budgetary constraints still limit the length of meetings and sessions, the membership of international fora grows ever larger. The membership of the United Nations has grown to encompass virtually the entire world, as these two maps illustrate:

- The World in 1945 (UN Map No. 4135 Rev. 3, May 2010)
- The World today (UN Map No. 4136 Rev. 12.1, July 2018)

For interpreters, the result has been faster and more difficult speeches, and the staffing strength of interpretation services cannot always keep pace. In former times, an ambassador conveying an important message was expected to speak slowly and deliberately. Today, he is often under pressure to speak fast because there are another 190 speakers awaiting their turn. The average rate of delivery of UN speakers today is 132 words per minute, sometimes rising as high as 170.

Researchers who study the relationship between the speed of speech and its comprehensibility put the 'normal' range of human speech at about 140–180 words per minute, but speech can easily attain speeds of 200 or 300 words per minute and remains roughly comprehensible even at 500 words per minute. Generally, only excited sportscasters or auctioneers reach such high rates of delivery, but many normal speakers do tend to speak very fast in certain situations, especially when they have several important points to make and are up against a strict time-limit. At these inordinate speeds, it is important for an interpreter to do everything possible to reduce the number of words and syllables the vocal apparatus must produce. Otherwise, one will fall prey not only to errors of language and meaning but also to errors of articulation or enunciation. Minimizing verbiage is also important because an interpreter must focus on ideas rather than words, and using a concise formulation enables you to get one idea out of the way so that your mind can focus on the next idea, improving your ability to get all of the meaning right. An interpreter rendering the translation of a poem at a leisurely, informal poetry reading would certainly strive to roughly replicate the structure, pace and form of the original as well as the ideas. But when speech reaches a certain speed of delivery, form and structure become secondary, as the interpreter's primary function is to get the gist of the meaning across. Today, a simultaneous interpreter must bear in mind at all times, even if (s)he is given a written text, that what (s)he is translating is not a literary composition but a live speech, the pace and density of which can suddenly increase at any moment. And it is helpful even for consecutive interpreters to be mindful of this, because neither speakers nor their audiences like to be kept waiting.

What does one do when the person speaking uncomfortably fast is an official delivering a formal policy statement? Besides the usual difficulties of translation and interpretation, a formal policy address poses some additional challenges. The first of these is the political status of the speech. A policy address is an official public statement of position, for the record. Such an address is usually delivered by a ranking government official, ambassador, a foreign minister, or the head of state or government and it is likely that the translated versions will be re-aired or reprinted. Consequently, as regards the content, nearly perfect accuracy is expected. Each and every idea must be correctly rendered. Secondly, there is the challenge of length. Such speeches can be very lengthy and detailed, since diplomats, ministers and heads of state will usually take the opportunity of a general debate to cover a great deal of ground. A third challenge is posed by the timeliness and diversity of the subject-matter. In one and the same address, the speaker may cover everything from environmental and demographic issues to human rights crises and regional conflicts in several parts of the world. This requires the interpreter to keep abreast of the latest developments in world affairs, as well as any related new concepts, technical terms, neologisms and jargon generated by the issues.

When rapid delivery makes it necessary for an interpreter to condense the speech in order to get across the essential elements of the message, certain non-essential features can be deleted, abridged, or treated by short references to what has already been said at full length. The leading candidates for this kind of compression are the redundant, the superfluous and the obvious. If a speaker repeats the same point several times in the same speech, the redundant repetitions can be deleted or abridged once the point has been made clear. Overabundant adjectives can also sometimes be compressed with no loss of meaning. Similarly, an item in a statement which is a matter of common knowledge or which the interpreter knows is already familiar to the audience may sometimes be sacrificed when the speaker's speed is such that 'something has to go' and there are other ideas in the statement which are more important or relevant. In other words, the wording and structure of a speech may have to be manipulated or modified, in ways that a translator would generally try to avoid, in order to preserve all of the essential ideas within the time limits dictated by the speaker's speed. Although the printed text of a formal policy statement, usually prepared long in advance, may follow the conventions of the written language, the interpreter's tools are drawn from the spoken language. In other words, the interpreter can – and often must – treat a speech as if it were being delivered extemporaneously even if it is a carefully prepared composition. The techniques an interpreter can use for this purpose can be categorized for the most part as compression and reformulation, since they seek to modify the text without altering the meaning.

The approach to live editing and condensing of a speech is somewhat different depending on whether the interpretation is done in the simultaneous or consecutive mode.

Example: Simultaneous

In the speech presented below, which was interpreted simultaneously, President Nestor Kirchner of Argentina covered a wide range of global and national issues in about 7.5 minutes, as a result of which he sometimes spoke at a relentless pace, with quite a few slips of the tongue, mispronunciations and numbers read out at high speed. The speech contains 1280 words spoken in 7.5 minutes so that the average speed of delivery is 170 words per minute, near the top of the so-called 'normal' range. The English interpreter was able to keep up and track this speech very closely because she had an English text provided by the speaker's delegation, but that is not always the case. In the left-hand column below is the English text provided by the speaker, which is a fairly literal, word-by-word translation of the Spanish original and contains all of his ideas, however awkwardly or wordily expressed. In the right-hand column is a proposed edited interpretation of this speech. Reformulations are highlighted. Due to the pressure of time, the speaker omitted some passages, but if the whole speech had been delivered, the suggested compression and reformulation would have saved about 222 out of 2,492 words, or about 9%. This may not seem like very much, but at these speeds even one syllable can make the difference between keeping up and falling behind. This comparison illustrates that, for purposes of simultaneous interpretation, using the 'closest idiomatic equivalent' produces a version consisting of segments that are both more natural and shorter – and hence more achievable in the simultaneous mode.

For purposes of comparison, listen to the brief statement below, spoken at a more measured rate of delivery, and consider the difference this makes for the interpreter. Notice also how a moderate rate of delivery makes it

ARGENTINA: Speaker's Translation	ARGENTINA: Interpretation
[bracketed italics = omitted on delivery]	
Mr. President,	Mr. President,
Five years ago	Five years ago
the governments **of our countries**	our governments
gathered **in this very site**	gathered **here**
hoping to work together	hoping to work together
in solving	to solve
some of the most **urgent and serious** problems	some of the most **pressing** problems
that our peoples **were – and still are – facing.**	**confronting** our peoples.
That is how the Millennium Declaration **arose**	**Hence** the Millennium Declaration
and, with it, a renewed **commitment** by the	**with its** renewed **commitment** by the
international community	international community
in favor of multilateralism and **respect for** human dignity.	to multilateralism and human dignity.
Concrete goals in development were favored, aimed at solving the imperative issue of	Concrete development goals were favored aimed at solving the imperative issues of
hunger, of poverty, **of** infant mortality rates, **of diseases** such as HIV/AIDS, **of** malaria and other **pandemics** and **of** social and juridical gender inequality.	hunger, poverty, infant mortality, HIV/AIDS, malaria and other **pandemics** and social and legal gender inequality.
The assessment of what we have achieved in these few years is far from satisfactory.	What we have achieved in these years is far from satisfactory.
The **severity** of the situation is, basically, the same.	The **gravity** of the situation is basically the same.
The modest advances in some issues cannot, **however**, weaken our will nor numb our conscience.	Modest advances on some issues cannot weaken our will nor numb our conscience.
Poverty, hunger and disease continue to afflict a vast **proportion** of women and men in the globe **to the point of obscenity.**	Poverty, hunger and disease continue to afflict a vast **share** of the world's women and men **to a repugnant degree.**

The absence of the rule of law and the massive **violations of human rights** in various	The absence of the rule of law and massive **human rights violations** in various places
cause great suffering and deepen political instability and civil conflicts.	cause great suffering and deepen political instability and civil conflicts.
The new and grave threats to international security	New and grave threats to international security
have permeated the whole spectrum of international debate.	**permeate** the whole international debate.
Poverty, social inequalities, injustice, social exclusion and the **estrangement** between expectations and reality	Poverty, social inequalities, injustice, social exclusion and the **gap** between expectations and reality
bring about an element of instability, working against the strengthening of democracy and development.	**inject** instability, working against the strengthening of democracy and development.
A large part of the problem lies, perhaps, in the **lack of correspondence** between declarations –**true expressions of wish**- and acts.	**Much** of the problem may lie in the mismatch between **words**, however truly felt, and **deeds**.
This is evident in two key matters: debt and international trade.	This is evident in two key areas: debt and international trade.
The persistence of discriminatory and inequitable policies in international trade	The persistence of discriminatory and inequitable policies in international trade
is **included in this list of** impediments of development,	is **among** these impediments to development,
both for the poorest nations and for middle-income countries such as **my own**, Argentina.	both for the poorest nations and for middle-income countries such as Argentina.
The prevalence of an ideological component in the policies of international credit	The prevalence of an ideological component in the policies of international credit
institutions is also distressing.	institutions is also distressing.
The so-called 'orthodox' **approach** that some are attempting to apply to **the issue of** indebtedness, an **approach** that has exhibited its shortcomings and inefficiency and that has worsened **the conditions of** poverty in the developing world,	The so-called 'orthodox' **approach** that some are attempting to apply to indebtedness, which has shown its shortcomings and inefficiency and worsened poverty in the developing world,
is **maybe** the area where the **prevalence of** this component becomes more evident.	**maybe** the area where this component is most **apparent**.
Economic development, security and human rights	Economic development, security and human rights
are the basic pillars of the United Nations,	are the basic pillars of the United Nations,
and therefore the simultaneous progress we may achieve in all three levels are the best guarantee for international peace and the well-being of humanity.	and the simultaneous progress we may achieve in all three is the best guarantee of international peace and the well-being of humanity.
With great effort, Argentina is managing to return to the path of development	**Arduously**, Argentina is managing to return to the path of development
and has achieved an **important** and sustained growth in its economy,	and has achieved **substantial** and sustained economic growth

while **at the same time** has succeeded in significantly reducing unemployment, poverty and destitution indexes.

while **still** succeeding in significantly reducing unemployment, poverty and destitution indexes.

After coming out from the crisis, indicators show a sustained growth in the economy and a **surplus situation in the fiscal and external accounts,** together with the recovery in **national** reserves.

With the crisis **behind us**, indicators show sustained growth in the economy and a **budget and trade surplus,** together with recovery in reserves.

Argentina has grown 8.8% in 2003, 9% in 2004 and over 9% during the first **semester** of 2005.

Argentina has grown 8.8% in 2003, 9% in 2004 and over 9% during the first **half** of 2005.

The consolidated primary surplus is 5% of the GDP

The consolidated primary surplus is 5% of GDP

and **the** reserves have increased **from** nearly 10 billion dollars to over 25 billion.

and reserves have increased nearly 10 billion dollars to over 25 billion.

Exports this year will exceed 40 billion dollars, with an estimated growth of about 15%.

Exports this year will exceed 40 billion dollars, with an estimated growth of about 15%.

[*The labor market shows **a declining trend in** unemployment, paired with a recovery in **salary levels,** a **pointed** improvement in the social situation and a clear decline in the poverty and destitution rates.*][omitted]

[*The labor market shows **declining** unemployment, paired with a recovery in **wages,** a **marked** improvement in the social situation and a clear decline in poverty and destitution rates.*][omitted]

Unemployment has dropped from 24% in 2003 to 12.1 over the first **semester** of 2005.

Unemployment has dropped from 24% in 2003 to 12.1 over the first **half** of 2005.

Poverty rates have dropped, from 57.5 to 40.2, and destitution rates have come down from 27.5 in 2003 to 15% 2004 and continue to decline.

Poverty rates have dropped, from 57.5 to 40.2, and destitution rates have come down from 27.5 in 2003 to 15% 2004 and continue to decline.

The improvement in salary levels in the real general salary index has reached 16%.

The improvement in **real wages** has reached 16%.

Since overcoming default, Argentina is consolidating as an opportunity for foreign investment.

Since overcoming default, Argentina is consolidating as an opportunity for foreign investment.

The primary education enrolment and the number of students starting the first grade are over 91.5% and 86.9%, the illiterate population is below 3%, and women's literacy rates are over 97.4%.

Primary education enrolment and the number of students starting the first grade are over 91.5% and 86.9%, the illiterate population is below 3%, and women's literacy rates are over 97.4%.

Women's participation is growing,

Women's participation is growing,

as a result women hold over 33% of seats at the House of Representatives and 43% of the seats at the Senate.

and women hold over 33% of seats in the House of Representatives and 43% of the seats in the Senate.

The infant mortality rates have dropped significantly, from 16.8 per 1000 to **the current** 13 per 1000.

Infant mortality rates have dropped significantly, from 16.8 per 1000 to 13 per 1000.

Public health programs are **implemented that extend** prevention to the whole of the population, drinking water supply and sewage systems are being increased, and through an agreement with Brazil, medicines shall be produced in order to cover the population infected with AIDS at an affordable price.

Public health programs are **extending** prevention to the whole of the population, drinking water supply and sewage systems are expanding, and through an agreement with Brazil, medicines shall be produced in order to cover the population infected with AIDS at an affordable price.

Regrettably, throughout this process of recovery, expansion and transformation, we did not have the support of the IMF,

which in turn had indeed supported until only weeks before the convertibility regime.

During its crisis, Argentina made net payments of about 13.5 billion dollars.

As many developing countries, we continue to endure both this archaic conception of the

indebtedness issue

and an international trade system that is unfair to agricultural products,

where subsidies and non-tariff barriers in developed countries continue to restrain our countries from their full growth based on their genuine resources.

In this sense, we call for the ministerial conference of the World Trade Organization

to be held at the end of this year in Hong Kong, China,

to fulfill the unfulfilled promise of placing development in the center of the international trade.

We follow attentively the international debate on the notion of sustainability of external debt.

We believe that international finances are too important to be left in the hands of concerted interests

that affect the stability of markets, discriminate against the small investor and spawn pro-cyclic policies.

That is why, in various fora, we have **put forward proposed modifications**

which increase **the** transparency **of** the international financial system,

which free this Organizations from certain financial lobbies, which bring an enhanced stability to the capital **flux** and which favor small investors.

There is neither ideology nor politics in this.

We **show** concrete facts **showing** that these Financial Organizations did not perform the role they must perform.

Looking ahead, our country has structured a debt-reduction strategy,

Regrettably, throughout this process of recovery, expansion and transformation, we did not have the support of the IMF,

which had indeed supported until only weeks before the **collapse**, the convertibility regime.

During its crisis, Argentina made net payments of about 13.5 billion dollars.

As many developing countries, we continue to endure both this archaic conception of the

indebtedness issue

and an international trade system that is unfair to agricultural products,

where subsidies and non-tariff barriers in developed countries continue to restrain our countries from their full growth based on their genuine resources.

Accordingly, we call for the ministerial conference of the World Trade Organization

to be held at the end of this year in Hong Kong, China,

to keep the unfulfilled promise of placing development at the center of international trade.

We follow **closely** the international debate on the concept of sustainability of external debt.

We believe that international finances are too important to be left in the hands of concerted interests

that affect the stability of markets, discriminate against the small investor and spawn pro-cyclic policies.

That is why, in various fora, we have **proposed changes**

which increase transparency **in** the international financial system,

which free this Organization from certain financial lobbies, bring enhanced stability to capital **flows** and favor small investors.

There is neither ideology nor politics in this.

Concrete facts show that these Financial Organizations did not perform the role they must perform.

Looking ahead, our country has structured a debt-reduction strategy, designed to gain degrees of independence in **the implementation of its** plans for **its** development and **the** growth of **its** economy.

designed to gain degrees of independence in **pursuing** plans for development and growth of its economy.

In this regard, we want to reaffirm our decision

In this regard, we want to reaffirm our decision

that payment of external financial commitments must not be made with detriment to resources pledged to social areas

that payment of external financial commitments must not be made to the detriment of resources pledged to social areas

such as education, health, housing and **employment promotion.**

such as education, health, housing and **job creation.**

We shall be firm in maintaining this position when dealing with the international credit

We shall be firm in maintaining this position when dealing with the international credit

organization,

organization,

and we reiterate our call for increased transparency, democracy and deep restructuring and revision of their policies

and we reiterate our call for increased transparency, democracy and deep restructuring and revision of their policies

in order to ensure their equity and efficiency.

in order to ensure their equity and efficiency.

In this line, Argentina has been since 2004 a co-sponsor in the UN Commission on Human Rights of **the resolution** on the 'Effects of structural adjustment policies and foreign debt on the full enjoyment of all human rights, particularly economic, social and cultural rights'.

Argentina has been since 2004 a co-sponsor in the UN Commission on Human Rights of the **resolution** on the 'Effects of structural adjustment policies and foreign debt on the full enjoyment of all human rights, particularly economic, social and cultural rights'

This resolution clearly deals with the **existing** link between external debt and the impossibility of full enjoyment of human rights.

which deals with the existing link between external debt and the impossibility of full enjoyment of human rights.

[TIME ALMOST UP]

[TIME ALMOST UP]

[omitted] [*We consider democracy **to be** a universal value that is not owned by any country or*

[omitted] [*We consider democracy a universal value not owned by any country or region,*

*region, and our government **directs its efforts towards** improving the quality of democracy, **reinforcing** the rule of law and ensuring the impartiality and independence of Justice, as well as implementing the international conventions on human rights which have been incorporated in our Constitution.*

*and our government **aims at** improving the quality of democracy, **strengthening** the rule of law and ensuring impartial and independent Justice, as well as implementing the international conventions on human rights which have been incorporated in our Constitution.*

*Argentina -**who** in the past endured systematic violations of human rights, characterized by the systematic use of torture, forced 'disappearance' and **summary extra-judicial** execution of its citizens-*

*Argentina -**which** in the past endured systematic violations of human rights, characterized by the systematic use of torture, forced 'disappearance' and **extra-judicial** execution of its citizens-*

*has given decisive steps in the internal judicial sphere to **put an end to** impunity **regarding** the authors of such atrocious crimes,*

*has taken decisive steps in the internal judicial sphere to **end** impunity **for** the authors of such atrocious crimes,*

***and** has **also** taken a proactive attitude to find the identities of its 'disappearance' victims.*

***and** has taken a proactive stance to find the identities of its 'disappearance' victims.*

In this perspective, Argentina joins the efforts by the international community to ensure that the persons responsible for crimes against humanity are brought before a court and punished.	**Here**, Argentina joins the efforts by the international community to ensure that the persons responsible for crimes against humanity are brought before a court and punished.
The International Criminal Court is an essential component in this struggle,	The International Criminal Court is an essential component in this struggle,
which we support and defend and whose integrity must be respected at all times.	which we support and defend and whose integrity must be respected at all times.
Argentina condemns terrorism in all its forms and manifestations, as a practice that affects the first fundamental right of every human being, the right to life.	Argentina condemns terrorism in all its forms and manifestations, as a practice that affects the first fundamental right of every human being, the right to life.
There can be no excuses for the indiscriminate attack on innocent civilians and	There can be no excuses for indiscriminate attacks on innocent civilians and
noncombatants, whatever the motive or grievance alleged to justify the act.	noncombatants, whatever the motive or grievance alleged to justify the act.
We stress that this fight, as all others, must be undertaken in **conformity** with international	We stress that this fight, as all others, must be undertaken in **keeping** with international
human right standards,	human right standards,
an indispensable condition to gain the legitimacy **that will guarantee our success.**	an indispensable condition to gain the legitimacy **and ensure success.**
Our country –that was the victim of two international attacks in 1992 and 1994, taking hundreds of human lives-	Our country, the victim of two international attacks in 1992 and 1994, taking hundreds of human lives,
has decided to play an active role in the struggle against international terrorism.	has decided to play an active role in the fight against international terrorism.
We are offered today a special opportunity to make an objective analysis on the functioning of our Organization after 60 years,	We have a special opportunity today to make an objective analysis of the functioning of our Organization after 60 years,
and to adopt the innovative and brave measures –**both at the normative and at the institutional levels**-	and to adopt the innovative and bold measures –**both normative institutional** -
that are needed to adapt the United Nations to the challenges that the new Millennium brings.	needed to adapt the UN to the challenges of the new Millennium.
We need a reform that is, first and foremost, on target and perdurable,	We need a reform that is, first and foremost, on target and sustainable,
and that leads us to a revitalized, **modern multilateralism, more fair and just.**	and that leads to a revitalized, **modern, more fair multilateralism.**
The rule of law, the respect for and promotion of human rights, peace and dignity for the peoples of the world, are pressing demands that we need to answer.	The rule of law, respect for and promotion of human rights, peace and dignity for the peoples of the world, are pressing demands that we need to answer.
The building of a new, fairer world order demands not only the reduction of inequality	The building of a new, fairer world order demands not only reduction of inequality
within our countries, but also among all countries.	within our countries, but also among all countries.
In turn, the building of a more democratic world order demands	In turn, the building of a more democratic world order demands

that all countries have	that all countries have
the chance to make a contribution,	the chance to make a contribution,
since only an authentically collective exercise contemplating the interests of all actors, big and small,	since only an authentically collective exercise contemplating the interests of all actors, big and small,
will enhance the legitimacy of any new design.	will enhance the legitimacy of any new design.
It is not through the reaffirmation of old privileges or the creation of new ones that this result will be accomplished	It is not by reaffirming old privileges or creating new ones that this result will be accomplished
- that would only **place a greater emphasis on** existing inequalities	- that would only **exacerbate** existing inequalities
between those countries with a greater economic, military and technological capacities, and all the rest.	between those countries with greater economic, military and technological capacities, and all the rest.
That is why we consider that any reform of the United Nations	That is why we consider that any reform of the United Nations
must **provide** the Organization **with** more transparency and democracy,	must give the Organization more transparency and democracy,
without creating new situations of privilege that would perpetuate the inequality between its members.	without creating new situations of privilege that would perpetuate inequality between its members.
In tense, troubled times as these, it is indispensable to reinforce international cooperation	In tense, troubled times like these, it is essential to strengthen international cooperation
and to avoid the lure of isolation and unilateral solutions.	and to avoid the lure of isolation and unilateral solutions.
There is no single nation or region able to handle by itself the sum of challenges and threats characterizing our times,	**No nation or region can by itself** handle the sum of challenges and threats of our times,
and only the multilateral work in this Organization and within **the framework of** regional and sub regional organizations can **allow us to attain the solution to** our shared problems.	and only multilateral work in this Organization and within regional and sub regional organizations can **lead to solving** our shared problems.
That is why we wish to renew our **participating vocation** and the search for enduring solutions,	That is why we wish to renew our commitment to **seeking participatory and enduring solutions,**
indispensable tools to ensure respect for the dignity of peoples.	**essential** tools to ensure respect for the dignity of peoples.
In this regard, allow me to pledge the full disposition of the Government of Argentina	In this regard, allow me to pledge the Government of Argentina's full readiness
for the United Nations to be able –through this reform- to fulfill the role it is called to play in this new millennium.	for the United Nations to be able –through this reform- to fulfill the role it is called on to play in this new millennium.
Our country aspires, as a result of this High Level Session,	Our country aspires, as a result of this High Level Session,
to hear the Heads of State	to hear the Heads of State
and Government of developed countries ratify their decision to fulfill the commitments made in favor of the sustainable development of the peoples in developing countries.	and Government of developed countries ratify their decision to fulfill the commitments made in favor of sustainable development for the peoples of developing countries.

In this context, Argentina shares the appeal to those developed countries that have not yet done so to set timeframes for the fulfillment by 2015 of the commitment to allocate 0.7% of their **gross national income** for official development assistance	In this context, Argentina joins in the appeal to those developed countries that have not yet done so to set timeframes for the fulfillment by 2015 of the commitment to allocate 0.7% of their **GNP** for official development assistance
and to ensure that such	and to ensure that such
assistance reaches as soon as possible those countries further behind in the fulfillment of the MDGs.	assistance reaches as soon as possible those countries furthest behind in the fulfillment of the MDGs.
The implementation of the right to development implies	**Implementing** the right to development implies
that each State must act to adopt sustainable development policies,	that each State must act to adopt sustainable development policies,
in accordance with the provisions of **the Summit of Johannesburg.**	in keeping with the provisions of **the Johannesburg Summit**.
In this field, Argentina **endeavors** to take the initiative	Here, Argentina **strives** to take the initiative
and to bring up in all international forums the **ethic** and equity dimensions	and to raise in all international forums the **ethics** and equity dimensions
that are essential to face local problems with global impact.	that are essential to face local problems with global impact.
Regarding the fulfillment of the human development goals set forth in the Durban Conference	Regarding the fulfillment of the human development goals set forth in the Durban Conference
and later in the Millennium Declaration,	and later in the Millennium Declaration,
achieving gender equality has a twofold function as an objective in itself and, at the same time, a tool to attain the other objectives.	achieving gender equality has a twofold function as an objective in itself and, at the same time, a tool to attain the other objectives.
From this perspective, we may point out that, in the field of the promotion and protection of women's rights and gender equality,	**Here**, we may point out that, in the field of the promotion and protection of women's rights and gender equality,
our country has achieved substantial progress.	our country has achieved substantial progress.
The empowerment of women and the progressive elimination of all forms of discrimination	The empowerment of women and the progressive elimination of all forms of discrimination
are **inescapable** components of the efforts by our governments, regional and international organizations and civil society organizations	are **key** components of efforts by our governments, regional and international organizations and civil society organizations
to promote sustainable development	to promote sustainable development
within the framework of inclusive societies, based on equity and full respect for human rights.]	within the framework of inclusive societies, based on equity and full respect for human rights.]
I wish to conclude by pointing out that the people of Argentina fervently expect the United Nations to help direct our destinies along the path of peace, justice and development.	**In conclusion**, the people of Argentina fervently expect the United Nations to help direct our destinies along the path of peace, justice and development.
Numerous resolutions by this General Assembly and its Decolonization Committee	Numerous resolutions by this General Assembly and its Decolonization Committee

have established that the question of the Malvinas, South Georgia and South Sandwich Islands

constitutes a special colonial Question that must be solved through bilateral negotiations

between my country and the United Kingdom.

The Decolonization Committee has made repeated declarations to this effect,

and we greatly value its action **in favor of seeking** a solution to this question.

We once again reaffirm the permanent willingness of our country

to reach a final, fair and

peaceful solution to this sovereignty dispute

which is a central **preoccupation** of the people of Argentina.

We therefore exhort the United Kingdom to promptly fulfill the call of the international

community to resume negotiations.

[SPEAKER'S TIME EXPIRED]

[*On the other hand, Argentina actively and constructively participates in favor of a new world order*

that can succeed in making globalization work for everyone and not for just a few,

allowing us developing countries to

increase employment creation, to raise the income level of the poorest and to provide a better access to education, health, housing and vital services.

It is crucial that we guarantee a sustainable development strategy with social inclusion.

Together with other countries which believe that the building of consensus is the best

way to preserve international peace and security,

*we trust more than ever in the future of this organization and in **the strengthening of** the multilateral system.*

We are ready to persevere until sense and solidarity finally prevail among nations.

*Only then will we know that **with our efforts we have been able to leave** to the next generations a better world that the one we were born into.*

This better world greatly depends on the courage, creativity and bravery each of us puts forward to lead change.

---

have established that the question of the Malvinas, South Georgia and South Sandwich Islands

constitutes a special colonial question that must be solved through bilateral negotiations

between my country and the United Kingdom.

The Decolonization Committee has made repeated declarations to this effect,

and we greatly value its action **in seeking** a solution to this question.

We once again reaffirm the permanent willingness of our country

to reach a final, fair and

peaceful solution to this sovereignty dispute

which is a central **concern** of the people of Argentina.

We therefore urge the United Kingdom to promptly fulfill the call of the international

community to resume negotiations.

[SPEAKER'S TIME EXPIRED]

[*Argentina actively and constructively participates in favor of a new world order*

that can succeed in making globalization work for everyone and not for just a few,

allowing us developing countries to

increase job creation, raise the income level of the poorest and provide better access to education, health, housing and vital services.

It is crucial that we guarantee a sustainable development strategy with social inclusion.

Together with other countries which believe that the building of consensus is the best

way to preserve international peace and security,

*we trust more than ever in the future of this organization and in **strengthening** the multilateral system.*

We are ready to persevere until sense and solidarity finally prevail among nations.

*Only then will we know that **through our efforts we leave** to the next generations a better world that the one we were born into.*

This better world greatly depends on the courage, creativity and courage each of us puts forward to lead change.

*It is **the** time to put utopias to work.*	*It is time to put utopias to work.*
*It is **the** time, **in summary**, to reduce the gap **that** separates declarations from acts,*	*It is time, **in short**, to reduce the gap **that** separates word from deed,*
finding a way to put the best ideas to work.]	*finding a way to put the best ideas to work.*]
Thank you	Thank you
2,492 words	2,263 words [222 words less]

An example of the style of delivery of this speaker may be found at the following link:
NESTOR KIRCHNER, President of Argentina
25 September 2003. Néstor Kirchner en su primer discurso en la Asamblea General de la ONU
https://www.youtube.com/watch?v=NvXBco0dOXQ

easier for the interpreter to cope with other oratorical challenges, such as the use in this case by Secretary General Guterres, of an unusual form of Spanish, 'Portuñol' (Spanish sprinkled with Portuguese words and pronunciations).

13 Jan 2018 – Declaración por parte del Señor Presidente de la República de Colombia, Juan Manuel Santos y el Señor Secretario General de la ONU, António Guterres a los medios de comunicación en el Palacio de Nariño en Bogotá, Colombia (13 de enero, 2018). LINKS:

YouTube: https://www.youtube.com/watch?v=bDQolF2Uqm8

URL: http://webtv.un.org/search/declaraci%C3%B3n-por-parte-del-se%C3%B1or-presidente-de-la-rep%C3%BAblica-de-colombia-juan-manuel-santos-y-el-se%C3%B1or-secretario-general-de-la-onu-ant%C3%B3nio-guterres-a-los-medios-de-comunicaci%C3%B3n-bogot%C3%A1-colombia-13-de-enero-2018/5709862993001/?term=&lan=Spanish&cat=Meetings%2FEvents&sort=date&page=3

Example: Consecutive

In the following example, the author was asked to interpret a lecture by Congresswoman Minou Mirabal of the Dominican Republic and was given an advance draft of the speech in Spanish to work with. By translating this draft before the event, the author was better able to keep up with the speech when it was delivered and to minimize interruptions. A consecutive interpreter has more control over the pace of delivery since the speaker will usually pause between segments of the speech, but the speaker should be kept waiting as little as possible. The reader may wish to see how this is done by going to the link below and playing back the speech.

'Violence against Women and the Example of the Mirabal Sisters' – Lecture Delivered by Minou Tavárez Mirabal, Representative to the Dominican Chamber of Deputies and daughter of Minerva Mirabal, November 6, 2006, at Middlebury College. Translated and interpreted by James Nolan.

Google drive link: https://drive.google.com/file/d/1LwvtEAAidm-QfH-mdMBR5H2UPLYMZjJ2N/view

3 Translatability and Untranslatability in Interpreting[102]

According to an anecdote that once made the rounds among United Nations interpreters, a young delegate attending his first UN General Assembly, upon hearing simultaneous interpreting in six languages for the first time, approached a conference officer and asked, 'This translation system is wonderful, where can I buy one?' While the anecdote may be apocryphal, it pointedly raises a persistent paradox: simultaneous interpreting is as widely misunderstood as it is widely used. The world relies upon simultaneous interpreting for international communication and decision-making. Without it, multilingual debates and negotiations, already hampered by many political and procedural hurdles, would slow to a crawl due to the need for everything to be repeated sequentially in all of the speakers' various languages, as in the days of the League of Nations. Since most listeners would understand only one of the several versions they would have to listen to, the stultifying effect on communication and dialogue is hard to overstate. Besides communication, interpreting supports specialization by enabling experts and representatives to be chosen based on their subject-matter expertise rather than their knowledge of a particular language, an issue addressed by Graham Fraser, Canada's commissioner of official languages, in his article, 'Our High Court Should be Bilingual.'[103] For an organization like the European Union, with 24 official languages,[104] multilingual debate in real time would be impossible.

Yet, despite its importance, many still do not understand the purpose of simultaneous interpreting and tend to confuse or compare it with translation (understandably, given the fact that some of what a translator does involves interpreting the text, and some of what an interpreter does involves translating the speech.) There is even speculation that machine translation combined with voice recognition technology could lead to a form of automated interpretation.[105] Of course, while machine translation has been gradually improving, the human brain, the most powerful of all computers, does it much better and has been doing so for some 74 years, at least since simultaneous interpreting was introduced at the Nuremberg trials.

However, confusion over 'translating' versus 'interpreting' goes beyond the everyday misuse of the two words or the idea that it is a mechanical act that can be replicated by computers. The real confusion stems from not appreciating that writing/reading and speaking/listening are two different ways of understanding, encoding, decoding and re-encoding ideas. One way works with visual/graphic or tangible symbols that are meant to be fixed or permanent, and the other works with aural symbols – the fleeting sounds of the human voice – which convey a vastly greater range of meaning, especially emotional meaning, and are constantly evolving. The fundamentally different nature of these two forms of symbolic communication can be glimpsed when one considers, for example, why it is that a libretto can be translated but an opera is rarely performed in translation.[106] Because written words originated as graphic representations of spoken words, we tend to focus on their semantic resemblance rather than on the differences between the pen and the voice as a medium of communication.

Although translational analysis plays a role in a wide range of cultural and social activities, four principal modes of translation (excluding sign language[107]) are widely practiced today:

- written translation
- sight translation
- consecutive interpretation
- simultaneous interpretation.

They differ in mode and scope of input and output. A complete picture of these modes of processing is given in the table below.

	Input (determined by pace of processing: intermittent or continuous)	Senses used	Output	Senses used
Written translation	Written gestalt – interpreter controls	Sight (reading): one or more pages at a time	Written: delayed	Touch, fine motor coordination, & Sight (writing, keyboarding)
Sight translation	Written gestalt – interpreter controls	Sight (reading): one page at a time	Oral: delayed	Sight & Voice (speaking)
Consecutive interpretation (without notes)	Auditory gestalt – speaker controls	Hearing: up to several sentences at a time	Oral: delayed	Voice (speaking) & Sight (observing the speaker)
Simultaneous interpretation (SI)	Auditory linear – speaker controls	Hearing: up to several words at a time	Oral: real-time	Voice (speaking)

It is possible for interpretation to take place without spoken words (e.g. sign language interpreting) or for translation to take place without written words (e.g. symbolic or picture writing). Meanings are transferred from one language/culture to another, i.e. from one system of meanings to another. When writing is used, the meanings are transmuted through written words. The words serve as fixed graphic symbols of the meanings in that system of meanings.

Meaning is contextual. It is in SI that the smallest quantum of incremental meaning is presented to the mind at a given instant. Thus, it is hardest for the mind to grasp and process.

For example, word choice, a key concern in written composition, takes on different parameters for an interpreter, who is often forced by timing to prefer the shorter of two possible words or phrases. An interpretation is not so much a composition as an improvisational performance. As with any other art, performers of simultaneous interpreting do not always do it perfectly but are nonetheless always expected to perform. As aptly put by Douglas Schuler, one of the co-authors of *Liberating Voices: A Pattern Language for Communication Revolution* (MIT Press), 'Totally accurate translation is impossible but imperfect translation is ubiquitous – and essential.'[108] Still, if it existed, would 'totally accurate' translation or interpreting be good translation or interpreting? Does an interpreter best convey a speaker's meaning and intent by striving to reflect each and every semantic nuance with 'total accuracy?' The problem is not that simple. Schuler goes on to offer an equally apt description of what good translation is and how it is shaped by context:

> Moreover, the context of the words in the sentence, the sentence in the paragraph, etc., that is being translated, all within the context of the inspiration and intent and audience are all relevant when translating. ... Translation, therefore, is not a mechanical act, but a skilled and empathetic re-rewriting or re-performing of a text or utterance or intention in which an understanding of the two cultures being bridged is essential.[109]

Because the re-performing of the message requires empathy, it must be done by another human being. Empathy enables the interpreter both to understand the speaker's ideas and to reflect faithfully the speaker's intent (as does contact with the speaker before the speech). How that empathy comes into play is an intuitive process that is difficult to describe, but which can be learned through practice, like acting or music.[110]

Perhaps the best way to gain a better understanding and appreciation of the simultaneous interpreter's task is through a closer look at the dynamic structure of the encoding process that takes place during an interpreted encounter. This is also a good way to explain why translation and interpreting require different tactics to render meaning. As Schuler states, such a performance is anything but mechanical.

A concisely formulated standard of good interpreting and translation that is often referred to in the codes of professional conduct of judicial interpreters states that interpreters and translators should 'faithfully and accurately reproduce in the target language the *closest natural equivalent* of the source language message [emphasis supplied].'[111] This definition does not say 'the nearest equivalent word.' 'Closest' refers to closeness of meaning, not necessarily of words. This is the first of three important considerations regarding the performance dimensions of translation and interpreting, outlined below.

Firstly, one must be careful to distinguish between meaning and words. Words are one means among many by which speakers and writers express meaning. Should a simultaneous interpreter attempt to track the wording of the original message? That can sometimes be done, and it is a useful strategy when interpreting an utterance resembling a quotation or dictum, but the effort it demands of a simultaneous interpreter can lead to omitting or distorting other parts of the message, especially when the syntax is complex or when a speaker's intent differs from his literal meaning (as often happens in diplomatic discourse), or when the connotations may be more important than the denotation (as happens in irony, allusions, or humor). As a measure of completeness, a word count can serve as a rough indicator of whether the entire text of a book has been translated from the source language into the target language, but it does not tell us whether a speaker has made his point to the intended audience.

Secondly, one must bear in mind the time constraints under which the communication takes place. Martin Luther took pride in the fact that, when translating the Bible, he sometimes spent up to four weeks researching a single word.[112] Such patience and intellectual discipline is commendable in a translator. But to a simultaneous interpreter with only seconds in which to produce an acceptable equivalent, obsessively searching for the most suitable word is a case of 'the best is the enemy of the good.'

Many novice interpreters fall victim to the *mot juste* syndrome, the need always to find exactly the right word or expression. Even an experienced interpreter will sometimes falter in mid-sentence, struggling to retrieve the ideal target-language word or phrase from memory and will still draw a blank. Simultaneous interpreting is expected to begin and end at the same time as the original speech so that the participants at the meeting can complete their business and adjourn. In simultaneous interpreting, time is of the essence, and a conference interpreter has to perform his or her task within the time limits dictated by the speaker and the setting. A media interpreter is subject to a similar constraint, since lagging behind the original speech could use up a few seconds of additional live broadcast time, which translates into a substantial additional cost[113] if the problem cannot be cured by editing.

Thirdly, one should remember how the content of the communication was created. Except in extemporaneous remarks, speakers generally prepare their speeches beforehand, memorize them or at least think them through, or speak from written notes or teleprompters. Therefore, the structure and style of the oral material the interpreter hears may bear a deceptive resemblance to written prose. But readers are not generally expected to absorb intelligently what they read at rates of up to 170 words per minute, while interpreters nowadays must sometimes keep up with speakers who deliver their speeches at that rate. A word or expression that might cause a reader to pause momentarily in order to reflect upon its meaning cannot be processed in that way by the interpreter. Thumbing through a dictionary is usually out of the question. Hence the importance to an interpreter of a general education broad enough to recognize any source language utterance and/or to derive the meaning from the context. The 'speeches' with which interpreters work are often writings read aloud, which means they are more complex and densely packed with meaning than spontaneous speech.

What is Translatable?

Working with material whose translatability is shaped by the performance dimensions just described, how much semantic content should a competent simultaneous interpreter be expected to render from the source to the target language? Opinions vary. According to one thorough study, conveying meaning from source to target language accounts for about 60% of the work done by parliamentary interpreters.[114] In some contexts, a 'goal' of 90% completeness is used. In some simultaneous interpreting examinations a passing performance is 'getting 70% of the meaning right.' Naturally, measuring and quantifying 'meaning' in devising these tests and standards is itself a complex matter. For instance, what if the 30% that was lost in an interpreter's 'passing performance' on an exam contained some of the speaker's main points (for example, because they came at the end and the interpreter fell behind while struggling with details)? Posing that question points up how arbitrary quantitative criteria can be and prompts the following propositions about simultaneous interpreting techniques:

(1) An interpreter should exercise sound editorial judgment in deciding what must be fully conveyed and what can be safely edited while keeping pace with the speaker and respecting the original meaning and intent; and

(2) A simultaneous interpreter should strive to convey all of the speaker's intended meaning by focusing on the main ideas, even if it requires systematically condensing verbiage and abridging or deleting details that are obvious, redundant or superfluous.

We know that there is often no exact one-to-one correspondence between words and structures in different languages.[115] This alone should suffice to immunize interpreters against the mental blocks induced by the *mot juste* temptation, since it shows that searching for 'the' equivalent is often futile. Whatever target language equivalent is used, it will probably not correspond completely to the source language item. The goal of complete accuracy in diction is often illusory. A more relevant point is that even within the confines of a single language, we commonly call things by more than one name or say things in different ways, depending on context and usage. Also, there are often two or more interchangeable ways of saying something (e.g. 'How are you?' and 'How are you doing?'; 'onerous' and 'burdensome'). An interpreter who has formed the rote habit of using a single target language equivalent is applying to the complex task of multilingual communication a constraint that he does not usually apply to the simpler task of monolingual speech. As a result, the interpreter will be hard-pressed if he or she forgets that one target language equivalent. One of the more perverse features of human memory is the fact that, especially as we grow older, certain simple everyday words tend to 'slip our minds' with no rhyme or reason.

Consequently, being mindful that memory is fallible, it is wise to start from the assumption that for any given source language item there may be several possible equivalents in the target language, depending on the context and circumstances. This means the interpreter will usually have choices. Having choices is an advantage, which is why interpreter training should include practice on 'widening the options.' The fact that context largely determines meaning has many implications for the interpreter's choices. Here are some examples.

(1) The context may modify or narrow the meaning of the source language wording, making it harder to retrieve an apposite target-language equivalent from memory.[116] In the following example, the context makes it necessary to use two target language verbs for one source language verb:

> 'A través de una acción integral basada en una estrategia de acompañamiento social y educativo personalizado, los menores aprenden castellano, practican actividades de ocio y tiempo libre, habilidades sociales tales como resolución de conflictos, comunicación y pensamiento crítico...'

> ['Through a comprehensive action strategy based on social support and personalized education, children learn Castilian, engage in recreation and leisure activities, and practice social skills such as conflict resolution, communication and critical thinking...']

Because the verb 'practice' does not work with the object 'recreation and leisure' in this context, it is necessary to use two verbs in English, although only one verb is used in Spanish.

(2) The context may make the meaning more generic, making it possible to use any of several roughly synonymous target-language items, thus making the interpreter's task easier. For example: 'The Mayor's office was flooded/deluged/inundated with complaints.'

(3) The context may point to simply using a standard word or phrase, such as a common idiom or cliché. For example: Nos hemos dilatado

mucho, ha llegado la hora de arremangarse la camisa. ('We've delayed too long, the time has come to roll up our sleeves').

(4) The general context (character of the audience, identity of the speaker, nature of the subject, etc.) may render some of the possible options inappropriate or 'taboo,' as in the case of politically correct speech, gender-neutral language, or in a speech to a specific age group. For example, the following sentence from a discussion of EU affairs inadvertently uses a comical ethnic stereotype by translating literally a French expression used to refer generally to English-speakers: 'An internal document…shows that 11 out of the 26 spokespersons who have already been designated to the incoming European Commission are Anglo-Saxon. Of these, seven are English and four are Irish.'[117]

(5) A given institutional context may require the interpreter to follow additional constraints or stylistic preferences. Most organizations have fixed conventions about terminology or jargon. Delegates at international gatherings sometimes monitor the interpreters, listening for the 'right' target language equivalents they expect to hear. Courts sometimes ask an interpreter to adhere to something like a 'verbatim' interpretation, and the interpreter may have no choice but to comply.[118] However, as one court interpreter has commented, 'While interpreting in the courtroom must admittedly adhere much more closely to the source, there is no reason why an interpreter cannot utter an idiomatic and faithful rendition while interpreting at the stand if he or she has good notetaking skills to back up a good memory and an intimate feeling and understanding of the languages involved.' In the diplomatic sphere, note-taking is an important skill used to preserve the gist of discussions and decisions taken at a meeting, but this type of note-taking is quite different from that of the interpreter and, since it is regarded as a clerical or secretarial function, those who do it do not necessarily receive the necessary training to produce a verbatim record. Diplomats and government officials do not always realize that the notes taken by an interpreter as an aid to short-term memory are of a completely different kind and do not lend themselves to reproducing specific wording. For example, when Madeleine Albright met for the first time with President Jimmy Carter and other members of his cabinet to discuss a sale of military aircraft, she was surprised to discover that she was expected to have kept detailed notes about what was said because she was the most junior person in attendance. Zbigniew Brezezinski summoned her after the meeting and asked 'Would you please consult your notes and tell Secretary Vance and Secretary Brown how the President phrased a particular point on the sale?'[119] The protocol expected by Mr. Brzezinski and his colleagues was that the note-taking task fell by default to the most junior person in the room. In an international context, this may be the most junior member of the delegation that is producing the memorandum of conversation, as in the example below.

THE WHITE HOUSE
WASHINGTON

~~TOP SECRET~~/SENSITIVE/
EXCLUSIVELY EYES ONLY   February 21, 1972

MEMORANDUM OF CONVERSATION

PARTICIPANTS: Chairman Mao Tsetung
                     Prime Minister Chou En-lai
                     Wang Hai-jung, Deputy Chief of Protocol
                       of the Foreign Ministry
                     Tang Wen-sheng, Interpreter

                     President Nixon
                     Henry A. Kissinger, Assistant to the President
                       for National Security Affairs
                     Winston Lord, National Security Council Staff
                       (Notetaker)

DATE AND TIME: Monday, February 21, 1972 - 2:50-3:55 p.m.

PLACE: Chairman Mao's Residence, Peking

Public domain image from website of the Nixon Foundation.
https://www.nixonfoundation.org/exhibit/the-opening-of-china/

Dealing with Untranslatability

Within any of these contexts, and others, an interpreter may encounter source language items that present various forms of 'untranslatability,' each of which may call for a different approach. Dealing with seemingly untranslatable utterances requires one to bear in mind that the same idea or emotion may find expression in different ways from one culture to another. It involves asking, for example, whether an utterance is one of the following:

- The expression of an emotion: For example, the Portuguese word *saudade* is roughly translatable as 'longing, yearning, nostalgia.' Rather than an awkward three-word paraphrase, the best solution, if the context permits, might be for the interpreter to express the emotion with a note of *saudade* in her voice.
- An abstraction: What is referred to in one language using abstract nouns may be more usually referred to in another language using concrete nouns (e.g. atención a la niñez y adolescencia = 'care of children and adolescents'). Some source-language abstract nouns may have several more specific target language equivalents. For example, *normas* in Spanish usually corresponds to laws, rules, guidelines, or standards in English. It is better to use the closest specific equivalent meant by the speaker than to generalize by interpreting the word as 'norms.' A related tactic is summarizing by generalization: using a general term in the target language to cover several specifics in the source language that are

too numerous to retrieve instantly or to utter during the time allowed, e.g. 'difteria, escarlatina, sarampión y varicela' > 'childhood diseases'.

- The title of a person: Titles, forms of address and honorific words reflect social status and their usage is a matter of custom, but they are not used in the same way in all languages. For example, it is customary in Mexico to refer to all teachers and master craftsmen as *maestro* or *maestra*, but in English no such honorific title is used for those people. Similarly, the title *maître* is used in French when addressing or referring to lawyers and notaries, but in English no similar title is used for that set of people, although lawyers are sometimes referred to as 'counselor'. The correct English equivalent in this case is the less deferential 'Mr.,' 'Mrs.,' or 'Ms.' (An interpreter can preserve the missing nuance by giving a note of deference to his voice.[120]) Governmental, academic, diplomatic and military titles pose similar problems, particularly for an interpreter, since the person being addressed or referred to is often present in the room.
- The name of a cultural institution: For example, the Scandinavian word *Ombudsman*, having no satisfactory English equivalent that conveys the specific features of the institution, has simply been assimilated unchanged into English and other languages. To an audience unfamiliar with the institution, a paraphrase such as 'community mediator' might be appropriate.
- A technical term: Technical terms acquire equivalents in different languages at different times through coinage and convention. Pending the adoption of a target-language equivalent, the source language term is often used for a period of time. For instance, the English term 'software' was used in French for years before the French term *logiciel* was coined and introduced. For this reason, interpreters need to keep up to date with recent technical coinages. When new coinages and neologisms are first introduced into a language, it is more likely to happen in speech than in writing, as writing is thought of as more permanent and codified.
- A figure of speech, such as a metaphor: For an interpreter, it is just as important to identify an utterance as a figure of speech as it is to understand what the utterance means. Otherwise, the interpreter may commit the misleading (and sometimes foolish) mistake of interpreting figurative language literally, thus losing or distorting the underlying message. For example, in a discussion among doctors or emergency medical technicians, it would be important for an interpreter to recognize the figure of speech *poner el dedo en la llaga* as a common metaphor (roughly equivalent to 'putting salt in the wound,') which carries the meaning 'to make things worse'. If the interpreter fails to recognize this phrase as a metaphor, he or she might otherwise take it literally and interpret it as 'putting a finger into the wound', which could cause confusion in a medical setting.

When dealing with these types of utterances an interpreter often has to ask questions like:

- Should I look for a different part of speech? For example, many ideas expressed in Spanish with nouns are more usually expressed in English with a verb: 'La mejora de nuestro sistema educativo requiere mayores esfuerzos.' = 'We should try harder to improve our educational system.'
- Is there anything in the target language culture that is thought of or talked about in a comparable way? For example, the English stereotype 'yuppie' is untranslatable as such because it is a recent coinage based on an English acronym for 'young urban professional,' but in some contexts the corresponding French stereotype *jeune cadre dynamique* would convey the correct image and the right degree of irony.

Dealing at high speed with a range of items that present interpreting challenges and are shaped by context in which they are spoken requires not only a high degree of language proficiency and cultural competency, but also versatile thinking, analytical judgment, and rhetorical aptitude – a combination of skills that is difficult to achieve. Relying on a tit-for-tat 'bilingual glossary' style of interpreting is not conducive to developing that set of skills. It is only through practice and experience that the simultaneous interpreter develops a repertory of solutions that can be brought to bear immediately as problems arise. Examining the fundamentals involved in the interpreter's art, it becomes clear why interpreting is not synonymous with translating. It is also easier to understand why computers still have a long way to go in their efforts to catch up to their human counterparts.

4 A Primer for Interpreting Trainees

There is no substitute for training under the tutelage of an experienced interpreter. However, insofar as that ideal situation is beyond the reach of a trainee at a given time, it is helpful to have some general guidelines and words of advice to follow. The following basic pointers were developed in response to questions frequently asked by the author's students at a series of interpreting seminars. Their focus is on achieving optimal quality and speed mainly in the simultaneous mode.

- **What did he Say?!** The speaker isn't clear? Ask yourself: Who is he? Why is he here? What would I expect him to be saying here today? What has he been saying so far, and what would be the next logical thing to say? Am I trying to be clearer than the speaker? Should I? If one utterance escaped you, immediately go on to the next. Sometimes, the idea or nuance that escaped you will come back later in the speech and you will get a second chance.
- **Deliver <u>the message</u>.** Focus on ideas and feelings, not words. You are not writing a composition. You are re-stating what someone else just said.
- **Meaning is contextual.** Each utterance is partly defined by the previous one. Each utterance lays the groundwork for the next one. Follow the thread of the speech, and try to exploit its coherence. Continuity must be your guide even in a lengthy meeting. When you are in the booth but not actively interpreting, learn to relax and recover without completely turning off your attention so that you have your finger on the pulse of the meeting.
- **Silence is golden.** Don't feel embarrassed by a momentary silence. Don't be afraid to keep quiet until you know what you are going to say. Don't blurt out the first thing that comes to mind if you feel uncertain. Wait for a full unit of meaning to take shape in your mind. Don't start what can't be finished. If the speaker uses pauses, do the same.
- **Don't embroider.** Don't 'fill in' or 'embroider' out of nervousness. Don't elaborate on the speaker's ideas, even if they inspire you or fill you with enthusiasm. You are like a juggler keeping seven apples in the air.[121] Do not try to throw in one more or you may drop them all.

65

- **Leave well enough alone.** If your interpretation was accurate and complete, don't try to improve upon it merely because something more elegant has occurred to you.
- **When is 'close' close enough?** When the gist of the meaning is there, you have done your job. Accuracy is relative. Translation is rarely 100% complete and simultaneous interpretation is an inherently imperfect product. Most people understand this and make allowances for it.
- **Brevity is the soul of wit.** When there is a choice, prefer the shorter way of saying something. Even if an utterance is easy and you feel you have the luxury to be wordy, the very next utterance may be inordinately fast, obscure or difficult and you will need all your concentration to deal with it. Immediately free up your mind to deal with whatever comes next.
- **Never panic.** Your memory is most efficient when you are calm. Stay cool and try to maintain a steady rate of delivery even when you are skating on thin ice. When dealing with a difficult speech, use a straightforward conversational tone as your 'baseline' tone. Never let your voice betray nervousness or comment on your own performance.
- **Use all the tools.** Words are only one way of conveying meaning. Use your voice's intonation and pitch to give words the right color and the speech the right tone and emphasis. When appropriate, also use gestures and body language.[122]
- **The Tortoise and the Hare** When you are 'racing' with a fast speaker, in pacing your rate of delivery, try to be the tortoise, not the hare. Don't fall too far behind the speaker or try to get ahead of him by being overconfident. Even if he speeds up or slows down, try to maintain a steady pace in your own delivery, taking one firm step at a time. At the end of the speech, finish your last sentence even if the speaker has finished slightly ahead of you; don't leave it hanging out of embarrassment.
- **Keep it simple.** Some ideas are not simple. Cope with genuine complexity as best you can. But do not be afraid to state simple ideas in simple terms and, whenever possible, try to simplify formulations that are needlessly elaborate or verbose, e.g. 'We cannot fail not to ignore…' > 'We must recognize…'.
- **There's more than one way …** To a simultaneous interpreter, literalism is a trap. Almost everything can be said in more than one way. If you can't think of one, use another. Keep a notebook where you jot down different solutions to interpreting challenges as they occur.
- **Don't correct yourself unnecessarily.** If you realize that something you just said was wrong, and you have time, admit your mistake and state your correction to the audience as soon as possible. But if what you

said was basically correct, don't be overzealous and correct yourself unnecessarily.

- **When should I apologize?** Only if you have misled the audience, which is most likely to happen when the speaker's source language is one that no one in the audience understands, so that the listeners are completely dependent on you, the interpreter, for the message. Consequently, that situation calls for a special effort on your part. A minor error or omission, a slip of the tongue, or a technical glitch does not require an apology, and a fastidious interpreter is needlessly distracting. In simultaneous interpretation, it is not unusual for such mistakes to happen and go unnoticed; and it is generally understood that this product cannot be perfect. But if a significant error can be corrected, by all means do so, with dignity, phrasing your apology in the third person, e.g. 'The interpreter apologizes. The speaker actually said…' In settings where a record is being produced, bring your mistake to the attention of the record-writers. It may also happen that the speaker or his/her institution may disagree with some aspect of the interpretation provided and subsequently issue a correction or clarification.[123]

5 An Overview of Interpreting Skills[124]

A – Listening

Active listening: Analyze and mentally summarize what you hear

For most of us, most of the time, listening feels like a passive activity, one in which we are 'on the receiving end.' However, in interpreting, you must imagine that you are engaged in a lively and important conversation with the speaker and that you must not miss a word of what is said because you want to be able to jump in at any point. Indeed, that is exactly what you do when you interpret, except that your side of the 'conversation' consists of restating what is said in another language to another person. Moreover, you must mentally summarize for yourself what you have been hearing in order to help you make sense of what is coming. Following the thread of the speech will shed light on parts that might otherwise be confusing or inaudible. Make it a habit to use notes to keep track of key points.

EXERCISE: Listen attentively to the recorded speech at the website given below and jot down key words and ideas, pausing occasionally. During the pauses, check the accuracy and completeness of your notes against the transcript of the speech.

Remarks by President Barack Obama at Cairo University, 6-04-09
Office of the Press Secretary
(Cairo, Egypt)

http://www.americanrhetoric.com/speeches/barackobama/barackobam acairouniversity.htm

https://www.youtube.com/watch?v=NaxZPiiKyMw&fs=1&hl=en%5FU S&rel=0

B – Visualizing

From the ear to the mind's eye: Visualize what you hear; a picture is worth a thousand words

> Ce que l'on conçoit bien s'énonce clairement,
> Et les mots pour le dire arrivent aisément.
> – Nicolas Boileau, 1636–1711

As Nicolas Boileau observed three centuries ago, what is clear in one's mind is easier to express clearly in words. A picture or concept formed in the mind's eye is more easily translated into the target language than the wording of the source language. This intermediate non-verbal step helps the interpreter to overcome many problems, especially the tendency to impose source-language syntax and structure on the target language rendition. Under the pressure of fast delivery, the temptation to simply follow the syntax of the original speech is very strong. But it is easier to resist that temptation if one is 'translating from a picture', as in the illustration below. This often enables the interpreter to produce a rendition that is more natural, shorter and clearer. If a complex statement inspires an absurd image in your mind, so much the better: it is widely thought that absurd images work better as mnemonic devices.

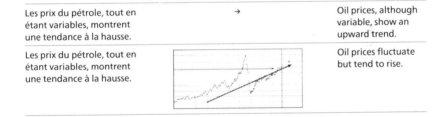

| Les prix du pétrole, tout en étant variables, montrent une tendance à la hausse. | → | Oil prices, although variable, show an upward trend. |
| Les prix du pétrole, tout en étant variables, montrent une tendance à la hausse. | | Oil prices fluctuate but tend to rise. |

Another way to describe this 'de-verbalizing' mental operation is to say that interpreting a speech involves two translations: first, the words of the original are translated into a mental image or engram; then, the mental image is translated into the words of the target language. So, the quality of the interpretation depends on how accurate a mental image of the original meaning is formed.

C – Public Speaking

> Frequent breaks will be necessary, because people can't concentrate as well when the message comes through the filter of an **interpreter's monotone**.
> – L. Barrington, *Mediating Across Cultures*

Practice in public speaking is an important part of training to become an interpreter for several reasons. First, many people studious enough to have acquired a thorough grasp of two or more languages tend to be somewhat introspective and, when faced with an audience, may freeze up and develop mental blocks or memory lapses. Second, interpretation assignments – especially the better ones – often require interpreters to perform before large audiences of important people, which can be rather intimidating even for those who are not shy. But stage fright can be overcome by the same method that actors use: rehearsal. Last but not least, an interpreter, like an actor, a talk-show host or a news announcer, has to learn how to use his or her voice.

In order to understand the kind of language used by public speakers and at international conferences, interpreters should appreciate how it differs from everyday speech. We use language in our daily lives primarily to communicate information and express feelings. But the main function of language as used by public speakers such as diplomats, officials, and corporate executives, who are usually acting as spokesmen for groups, is advocacy. A campaign speech by a candidate for office is designed to win the listeners' votes. A speaker praising a public figure is seeking to persuade listeners of that person's merits. An official making a public explanation or apology for an error or embarrassment is trying to persuade the public to forgive and forget. A diplomat making a lengthy policy statement is trying to persuade other diplomats to support her positions by striving to portray her country and its policies in a favorable light. Even a speaker using expository language to relate facts or report information is often doing so in order to support a particular viewpoint, thesis, or proposal.

Public speakers have usually acquired some proficiency in the art of persuasion, and interpreters must be able to mirror that skill. So, interpreters should strive to be good public speakers. An important step in becoming an effective public speaker is learning not only to use one's skill at expository and descriptive speech but also to draw on one's powers of persuasion. Cultivating that skill will also help the interpreter to acquire greater confidence and overcome stage fright.

If you feel overawed by a particular interpreting assignment, pause to size up your audience: Do they know what to expect from an interpreter? Are they monitoring you? Will they judge you? By what standard? Given the importance of the speech or the speaker, will they even notice you, other than to hear your rendition of the speech and catch the gist of the meaning? Are they experts? Most people understand the difficulty of simultaneous interpretation and are not expecting perfection. Experts will usually have had previous exposure to conference interpreting, understand its limitations, and will not be misled by a slip of the tongue. On the other hand, if audience expectations are high, you should be aware of that and strive to give satisfaction. A speaker who understands the target language will sometimes make adjustments in his speech in light of what he hears the interpreter doing, e.g. by moderating his rate of delivery or by repeating an important point until he hears the interpreter render the desired nuance.[125]

Cultivate a constructive rapport with your audience by showing intellectual humility and professional pride. Regarding the subject of the meeting, keep an open mind and remember that there are two sides to every issue. Maintain a low profile, especially when you are not very familiar with the subject matter. Learn all you can from each speaker and from interactions with the meeting participants and audience. If you have managed to learn some of the specialized jargon of a technical meeting, use it as needed but do not go out of your way to display of your new-found expertise, as it will then be all the more embarrassing if you make a mistake.

Trainee interpreters should take every opportunity to develop their speaking skills and to ward off stage fright by participating in activities that involve appearing before an audience, such as community associations and clubs, public speaking societies like Toastmasters, or amateur theatre groups.

Remember that preparation is vital to self-confidence. Know the issues and terminology of the gathering. Know the speaker. Know his purpose at the meeting. Get a copy of the speech or notes and annotate it. Whenever possible, pre-translate difficult segments of a speech, such as quotations.

Remember that interpreting is a form of public speaking and interpreting for international conferences, with participants coming from many different nations and cultures and with the output being recorded and eventually broadcast worldwide, is a form of acting on the world stage. Above all else what is expected of you by an international audience, and by the other interpreters who may be taking relay from you, especially if your target language is a lingua franca like English, is clarity. This means cultivating a relatively neutral style of speech unencumbered by strong accents or regionalisms. In this regard, there is no better advice than that offered by a great actress and acting teacher, Uta Hagen:

> Hamlet's advice to the players, 'Speak the speech, I pray you, as I pronounced it to you, trippingly on the tongue,' does not make much sense when delivered with New Yorkese distortions. We have heard the comic overtones, the disservice done to the poetry of Christopher Fry and T. S. Eliot, to the tirades of Shaw by drawls and twangs and slurs. Nor is British speech the answer. It places Chekhov, Ibsen, Strindberg or Molière in the heart of England. British speech belongs to our colleagues abroad. If it is demanded by a specific character or the milieu of the play, it can be learned with the relative ease with which other dialects or accents are learned for particular roles.[126]

D – Multitasking

Listening and speaking

If someone interjects responses while I am going through an important statement, I may choose not to stop but will nevertheless register the content of those responses even as I go ahead with my speech. This common ability to listen to someone else even as we are speaking is one we all possess but are taught not to use out of courtesy. An interpreter, however, must learn by practice how to use it systematically.

EXERCISE: Shadowing. Choose a recorded speech from one of the repositories listed below. Listen to the recording through earphones and repeat after the speaker without falling behind. Record yourself, then listen to the recording with a critical ear. Repeat the exercise and see whether your delivery improved the second time.

Speaking and thinking

EXERCISE: Shadowing. Listen attentively to a speech from one of the repositories listed below and repeat after the speaker without falling behind. At the end of the speech, verbally summarize as best you can the gist of the speech while recording yourself. After a break, play both the speech and your summary, and see whether anything important was omitted from your summary.

Online speech repositories

European Commission/SCIC Speech Repository: https://webgate.ec.europa.eu/sr/
http://ec.europa.eu/dgs/scic/cooperation-with-universities/speech_repository.htm

EMCI Speech Repository: https://webgate.ec.europa.eu/sr/

UN Webcast: http://www.un.org/webcast/ga/58/debate-23.htm
http://webtv.un.org/watch/france-general-debate-67th-session/1861072592001/

English presidential speeches: http://millercenter.org/president/speeches

IMF webcast: http://www.imf.org/external/mmedia/index.aspx

James Nolan YouTube Channel, French speeches:
https://www.youtube.com/playlist?list=PLINLWjJMZwUNcPxhv9hDfp5zCFGFi7x47

James Nolan YouTube Channel, Spanish speeches:
https://www.youtube.com/playlist?list=PLINLWjJMZwUPb3M6qGRt2M3txSQJQ_088

World Economic Forum (WEF) annual meeting 2018:
https://www.weforum.org/events/world-economic-forum-annual-meeting-2018

World Economic Forum (WEF) annual meeting 2019:
https://www.weforum.org/events/world-economic-forum-annual-meeting-2019

American Rhetoric Speech Bank: http://www.americanrhetoric.com/speechbank.htm

Interpreter Training Resources: http://interpreters.free.fr/links/practicematerial.htm

Speaking, reading and thinking

EXERCISE: Shadowing. Listen to the following recordings and repeat after the speakers without falling behind. As you do so, follow along in the transcripts (below) and underline key words and main points. At the end of each speech, write out a summary of the main points and ensure that you have a satisfactory translation for all key words.

Statement by Canadian Prime Minister **Stephen Harper** *at the* World *Economic Forum; 26 January 2012; Davos, Switzerland*

https://dumpharper.wordpress.com/harper/the-speeches/harper-2012-world-economic-forum-davos/

'Thank you Professor Schwab for that kind introduction, I also want to thank you particularly for the invitation to speak here that you extended to me earlier this year. But more than that, Professor, you have made the World Economic Forum an indispensable part of the global conversation among leaders in politics, business, and civil society. And in the face of continuing global economic instability, the opportunity this gathering provides is now more valuable than ever. So I know everyone here joins me in thanking you for, in service of the common good, your vision and your leadership.

My Greetings to Ambassador Santi; to the Governor of the Bank of Canada, known internationally as Chair of the Financial Stability Board, Mark Carney; to our hard-working Minister of International Trade, Ed Fast; and to the best finance minister on the planet, Jim Flaherty. And let me just say that I'm especially proud to see so many outstanding Canadian business leaders making their presence felt here in Davos.

Ladies and gentlemen, I will use my time today to highlight Canada's economic strengths and to frame the choices we face as we work to secure long-term prosperity for our citizens in a difficult global environment that is likely to remain so.

As you know, Canada has economically outperformed most industrialized countries during these recent difficult years for the global economy.

Forbes magazine ranks Canada as the best place on the planet for businesses to grow and create jobs. The OECD and the IMF predict our economy will again be among the leaders of the industrialized world over the next two years.

And, one more cherished accolade, of course, is that for the fourth year in a row, this body, the World Economic Forum, says our banks are the soundest in the world.

These evaluations are the result of sound fundamentals. Among G-7 countries, Canada has the lowest overall tax rate on new business investment. Our net debt-to-GDP ratio remains the lowest in the G-7 – and by far.

And, while we remain concerned about the number of Canadians who are still out of work, Canada is one of only two G-7 countries to have recouped all of the jobs lost during the global recession.

Indeed, more Canadians are now working, than before the downturn. How was this achieved?

Faced with the worst global economic crisis since the 1930s, our Government implemented some of the most extensive and targeted economic stimulus measures of the G-20.

We made historic investments in infrastructure. We encouraged businesses to invest and helped them to avoid layoffs. We put substantial funding into skills training, and we extended support for workers who lost their jobs.

These things we did on a timely, targeted and temporary basis. We did not create permanent new programs or government bureaucracy. As a consequence, our deficit is now falling, our debt-GDP ratio has already peaked and we do not need to raise taxes. I should add that we also did not reduce immigration or give in to protectionism.

Instead, we have maintained the high levels of immigration that our ageing labour force of the future will require. We have continued to pursue new trade agreements.

And we have taken action to make Canada, among G-20 countries, the first tariff-free zone for manufacturers. We have pursued these policies, Ladies and gentlemen, because our number-one priority as a government is prosperity, that is, economic growth and job creation.

Now, that may sound obvious, almost clichéd. But is it really? As I look around the world, as I look particularly at developed countries, I ask whether the creation of economic growth, and therefore jobs, really is the number-one policy priority everywhere?

Or is it the case, that in the developed world too many of us have, in fact, become complacent about our prosperity, taking our wealth as a given, assuming it is somehow the natural order of things, leaving us instead to focus primarily on our services and entitlements?

Is it a coincidence that as the veil falls on the financial crisis, it reveals beneath it, not just too much bank debt, but too much sovereign debt, too much general willingness to have standards and benefits beyond our ability or even willingness to pay for them?

I don't know. But what I do know is this. First, that the wealth of western economies is no more inevitable than the poverty of emerging ones, and that the wealth we enjoy today has been based on – and only on – the good, growth-oriented policies, the right, often tough choices and the hard work done in the past.

And second, that regardless of what direction other western nations may choose, under our Government, Canada will make the transformations necessary to sustain economic growth, job creation and prosperity now and for the next generation.

That further means two things: making better economic choices now and preparing ourselves now for the demographic pressures the Canadian economy faces.

On what we must do now, first, we will, of course, continue to keep tax rates down. That is central to our Government's economic vision. But we will do more, much more. In the months to come our Government will undertake major transformations to position Canada for growth over the next generation.

For example, we will continue to make the key investments in science and technology necessary to sustain a modern competitive economy. But we believe that Canada's less than optimal results for those investments is a significant problem for our country.

We have recently received a report on this – the Jenkins Report – and we will soon act on the problems the report identifies.

We will continue to advance our trade linkages. We will pass agreements signed, particularly in our own hemisphere, and we will work to conclude major deals beyond it.

We expect to complete negotiations on a Canada-EU free trade agreement this year. We will work to complete negotiations on a free trade agreement with India in 2013. And we will begin entry talks with the Trans-Pacific Partnership, while also pursuing other avenues to advance our trade with Asia. Of course, I will again be making an official visit to China very shortly.

We will also continue working with the Obama administration to implement our joint "Beyond the Border" initiative – our plan to strengthen and deepen our economic and security links to our most important partner.

However, at the same time, we will make it a national priority to ensure we have the capacity to export our energy products beyond the United States and specifically to Asia. In this regard, we will soon take action to ensure that major energy and mining projects are not subject to unnecessary regulatory delays – that is, delay merely for the sake of delay.

This complements work we are already doing, and that we will move forward on, with the Canadian Federation of Independent Business to cut the burden of red tape on entrepreneurs.

We will also undertake significant reform of our immigration system. We will ensure that, while we respect our humanitarian obligations and family reunification objectives, we make our economic and labour force needs the central goal of our immigration efforts in the future.

As I said earlier, one of the backdrops for my concerns is Canada's ageing population. If not addressed promptly this has the capacity to undermine Canada's economic position, and for that matter, that of all western nations, well beyond the current economic crises.

Immigration does help us address that and will even more so in the future. Our demographics also constitute a threat to the social programs and services that Canadians cherish. For this reason, we will be taking measures in the coming months, not just to return to a balanced budget in the medium term, but also to ensure the sustainability of our social programs and fiscal position over the next generation.

We have already taken steps to limit the growth of our health care spending over that period. We must do the same for our retirement income system. Fortunately, the centerpiece of that system, the Canada Pension Plan, is fully funded, actuarially sound and does not need to be changed. For those elements of the system that are not funded, we will make the changes necessary to ensure sustainability for the next generation while not affecting current recipients.

Let me summarize by saying, ladies and gentlemen, that, notwithstanding Canada's many advantages, we remain very concerned about the continuing instability of the global economy of which we are a part. The problems afflicting Europe, and for that matter, the United States, are not only challenging today but, in my judgement, threaten to be even greater problems in the future.

Having said that, each nation has a choice to make. Western nations, in particular, face a choice of whether to create the conditions for growth and prosperity, or to risk long-term economic decline. In every decision, or failure, to decide we are choosing our future right now.

And, as we all know, both from the global crises of the past few years and from past experience in our own countries, easy choices now mean fewer choices later. Canada's choice will be, with clarity and urgency, to seize and to master our future, to be a model of confidence, growth, and prosperity in the 21st century.

Thank you, ladies and gentlemen, for your kind attention.'

*After leading his party to a majority government, **Justin Trudeau** gave the following speech in Montreal. French is in italics.*

https://www.youtube.com/watch?v=xKWyk86yWsQ

Transcript from: *Maclean's, 20 October 2015*

Merci. Merci. Thank you. Thank you, my friends. *Merci. Merci, mes amis.* Thank you. Thank you, my friends. Yes.

Il y a – il y a plus de 100 ans, un grand Premier ministre, Wilfrid Laurier, a parlé des voies ensoleillées. Il savait que la politique peut être une force positive, et c'est le message que les Canadiens ont envoyé aujourd'hui. Les Canadiens ont choisi le changement, un vrai changement.

Sunny ways, my friends, sunny ways. This is what positive politics can do. This is what a causative, hopeful – a hopeful vision and a platform and a team together can make happen. Canadians – Canadians from all across this great country sent a clear message tonight. It's time for a change in this country, my friends, a real change.

Il y a tellement de gens à remercier ce soir et je vais passer beaucoup de temps dans les jours à venir à les remercier, mais je veux commencer par ma famille. J'aimerais, d'abord, remercier ma famille — Sophie, Xavier, Ella-Grace et Hadrien. Merci de m'avoir permis de servir. Merci, Sophie, pour ta force, pour ta compassion, pour ta grandeur d'âme et pour ta générosité profonde. Et à Xavier, Ella-Grace et Hadrien qui font dodo maintenant mais qui seront avec nous demain matin, mes enfants, on embarque dans une nouvelle aventure ensemble et je peux vous dire maintenant qu'il va avoir des moments difficiles pour vous en tant qu'enfants de Premier ministre, mais papa sera là pour vous, comme vous savez bien.

Je veux aussi remercier les gens qui me font confiance depuis 2008 — les gens de Papineau. Merci encore une fois de votre appui. Merci de votre confiance. Je serais, d'abord et avant tout, fier de vous représenter à la Chambre des communes. Vous, mes chers concitoyens de Papineau, vous m'aviez parlé des enjeux qui sont importants pour vous. Je vous ai entendus et cela m'a aidé à devenir un meilleur député, à devenir un meilleur chef, et cela va m'aider à devenir un meilleur Premier ministre. Merci.

I also want to specifically thank my good friends Katie Telford and Gerald Butts. Katie and Gerry are two of the smartest, toughest, hardest working people you will find anywhere. They share with me the conviction that politics doesn't have to be negative and personal to be successful, that – that you can appeal to the better angels of our nature, and you can win while doing it.

Tonight, my very good friends, we proved that. I hope it is an inspiration to like-minded people to step up and pitch in, to get involved in the public life of this country and to know that a positive, optimistic, hopeful vision of public life isn't a naive dream; it can be a powerful force for change.

And I also want to thank the incredible volunteers that made tonight happen. Over 80,000 Canadians got involved in the core of this campaign. They knocked on their neighbours' doors. They made phone calls. They sent emails. Hundreds of thousands more supported us actively with their friends and online. They convinced their neighbours and their families. And all of these people had one thing in common: they care deeply about their families, their communities and their country. They believe that better is possible and that active citizens can play a real part in making it happen.

Now this movement we've built was fuelled by these amazing volunteers, and from the bottom of my heart, I thank you.

Now I want to take a moment to speak about my colleagues across the aisle. Tonight, I received phone calls from all of them, including from Mr. Harper. Stephen Harper has served this country for a decade, and as with anyone who has devoted their life to this country, we thank him for his service.

Now over the course of this campaign, I had the opportunity to have a couple of brief personal conversations with him about our families. It reminded me of the extraordinary and unique sacrifices that are made by anybody who serves this country at the highest levels, and I want to remind everyone, as I've said many times over the course of this campaign: Conservatives are not our enemies, they're our neighbours. Leadership is about bringing people of all different perspectives together.

Je veux aussi rendre hommage à Thomas Mulcair qui a mené une campagne vigoureuse. Il s'est battu jusqu'à la fin. Aux militants de son parti, je comprends votre déception ce soir. Notre parti a vécu des moments difficiles il y a pas si longtemps. Alors ne vous découragez pas. Notre pays a besoin de citoyens engagés comme vous. Notre pays en sera plus fort. Merci.

Now you're all going to hear a lot tonight and tomorrow about me and about our campaign. Lots of people are going to have lots of opinions about why we were successful. Well, for three years, we had a very old-fashioned strategy. We met with and talked with as many Canadians as we could, and we listened. We won this election because we listened. We did the hard work of slogging it across the country. We met with hundreds of people in the dead of winter in the Arctic and with thousands of people in Brampton in the middle of this campaign.

You built this platform. You built this movement. You told us what you need to be successful. You told us what kind of government you want, and we built the plan to make it happen. In coffee shops and in town halls, in church basements and in gurdwaras you gathered. You spent time together with us, and you told us about the kind of country you want to build and leave to your children.

Vous nous avez fait part de vos défis dans votre vie de tous les jours. Vous nous avez dit que ça devenait de plus en plus difficile de joindre les deux bouts et de payer les factures à la fin du mois. Vous nous avez dit que vous étiez inquiets pour votre retraite. Vous nous avez dit que vos communautés avaient besoin d'investissement. Vous nous avez dit que les bons emplois se faisaient de plus en plus rares. Vous êtes l'inspiration derrière notre programme. Vous êtes la raison pour laquelle nous avons travaillé si fort pour nous rendre là où nous sommes ce soir. Et vous serez toujours au coeur du gouvernement que nous allons former.

Over the past three years, you told us what you're going through. You told us that it's getting harder and harder to make ends meet, let alone to get ahead. You told us you're worried about whether you'll be able to afford a dignified retirement. You told us that your communities need investment. You told us you need a fair shot at better jobs. You are the inspiration for our efforts. You are the reason why we worked so hard to be here tonight, and you will be at the heart of this new government.

So my message to you tonight, my fellow citizens, is simple: have faith in yourselves and in your country. Know that we can make anything happen if we set our minds to it and work hard.

Ce n'est pas moi qui a fait l'histoire ce soir, c'est vous. Ne laissez pas les gens vous dire le contraire. Je sais que je suis ici ce soir pour une seule raison : parce que vous m'avez choisi.

I didn't make history tonight; you did. And don't let anyone tell you any differently. I know that I am on stage tonight for one reason and one reason only: because you put me here. And you gave me clear marching orders. You want a government that works as hard as you do, one that is focussed every minute of every day on growing the economy, creating jobs and strengthening the middle class, one that is devoted to helping less fortunate Canadian families work their way into the middle class.

You want a Prime Minister who knows Canada is a country strong, not in spite of our differences, but because of them, a PM who never seeks to divide Canadians, but takes every single opportunity to bring us together. You want a Prime Minister who knows that if Canadians are to trust their government, their government needs to trust Canadians, a PM who understands that openness and transparency means better, smarter decisions. You want a Prime Minister that knows that a renewed nation-to-nation relationship with indigenous peoples that respects rights and honours treaties must be the basis for how we work to close the gap and walk forward together.

À mes compatriotes québécois, ce soir, ensemble, nous avons choisi la voie de l'engagement. Nous avons choisi de se réengager dans une politique plus rassembleuse, plus positive. Nous avons choisi de se réengager dans la gouverne d'un pays pour qui reflète nos valeurs et nos ambitions. Nous avons choisi de faire confiance et d'investir ensemble dans notre avenir.

Au cours des trois dernières années, j'ai passé beaucoup de temps à aller à votre rencontre et à vous écouter. Vous m'aviez dit que vous vouliez un gouvernement ouvert et transparent, un gouvernement qui fait confiance en ses citoyens, un gouvernement au service de tous les Canadiens et les Canadiennes. Ce soir, c'est l'engagement que je prends devant vous : je serai le Premier ministre de tous les Canadiens. Nous formerons un gouvernement intègre qui respectera les institutions et qui fera de la collaboration avec les provinces le principe premier de ses actions.

Chers amis québécois, merci. Ce soir, le Canada retrouve un peu de lui-même. Ce soir, le Québec fait un véritable retour au gouvernement du Canada.

Canadians – Canadians have spoken. You want a government with a vision and an agenda for this country that is positive and ambitious and hopeful. Well, my friends, I promise you tonight that I will lead that government. I will make that vision a reality. I will be that Prime Minister.

In this election, 1,792 Canadians stepped up, put their names on ballots and on lawn signs and ran for office. Three hundred and thirty-eight of them were chosen by you to be their voices in Ottawa, and I pledge tonight that I will listen to all of them.

There are a thousand stories I could share with you about this remarkable campaign, but I want you to think about one in particular. Last week, I met a young mom in St. Catharines, Ontario. She practises the Muslim faith and was wearing a hijab. She made her way through the crowd and handed me her infant daughter, and as she leaned forward, she said something that I will never forget. She said she's voting for us because she wants to make sure that her little girl has the right to make her own choices in life and that our government will protect those rights.

To her I say this: you and your fellow citizens have chosen a new government, a government that believes deeply in the diversity of our country. We know in our bones that Canada was built by people from all corners of the world who worship every faith, who belong to every culture, who speak every language.

We believe in our hearts that this country's unique diversity is a blessing bestowed upon us by previous generations of Canadians, Canadians who stared down prejudice and fought discrimination in all its forms. We know that our enviable, inclusive society didn't happen by accident and won't continue without effort. I have always known this; Canadians know it too. If not, I might have spoken earlier this evening and given a very different speech.

Have faith in your fellow citizens, my friends. They are kind and generous. They are open-minded and optimistic. And they know in their heart of hearts that a Canadian is a Canadian is a Canadian.

Mes amis, nous avons battu la peur avec l'espoir. Nous avons battu le cynisme avec le travail acharné. Nous avons battu la politique négative avec une vision rassembleuse et positive.

My friends, we beat fear with hope. We beat cynicism with hard work. We beat negative, divisive politics with a positive vision that brings Canadians together. Most of all, we defeated the idea that Canadians should be satisfied with less, that good enough is good enough and that better just isn't possible. Well, my friends, this is Canada, and in Canada better is always possible.

Thank you. Thank you very much. *Merci. Merci. Merci.*

Self-monitoring

While interpreting, it is helpful to listen to yourself occasionally as a spot-check on voice quality, accuracy, completeness and clarity of delivery. In simultaneous, this can be done by taking one earphone pad slightly off the ear momentarily so that you can hear your own voice as well as that of the speaker. In consecutive, it is best to record yourself for a brief time and review your performance later. Requesting candid reactions from peers is another way to obtain valuable feedback.

EXERCISE: Shadowing. Choose a recent speech from one of the repositories listed above, listen to it through earphones and repeat after the speaker without falling behind. Record your performance. Then play back your performance and analyze your delivery to spot any gaps, slips, errors, stumbles, hesitations, omissions or mispronunciations. If there were any, repeat that part of the speech aloud.

E – Coping with Speed of Delivery

Accuracy and completeness

The problem: speed + difficulty = error

The rate of delivery of a speech is a major factor affecting accuracy and completeness in interpretation. Excessive speed of delivery is common for several reasons. Some speakers, lacking experience of public speaking, tend to speak too fast out of nervousness. Sometimes, if a speech contains unpleasant or unwelcome aspects, or arguments about which the speaker does not feel confident, the speaker is anxious to get them out of the way. And some speakers seem to feel that their duty as a spokesman making public an official position has been adequately satisfied by providing the written text of the statement, so that the oral delivery is merely a formality that they can quickly discharge.

At the United Nations, in the yearly edition of the Delegates' Handbook speakers are now asked to deliver their speeches at a normal speed:

Statements made in any of the six official languages of the United Nations are interpreted into the other official languages: for written statements, it is essential that the delegations provide interpreters with copies of their texts to the Meetings Servicing Assistant in order to ensure the quality of the interpretation. ... Speakers are requested to deliver the statement at a speed that is interpretable. [*Delegates' Handbook*, 2016. Page 30.]

The recommended rate of delivery is about 120 words per minute. Unfortunately, this advice is not always followed, which is unfortunate since moderate speed of delivery makes it possible to get across even very difficult or complicated matters.

Consider the following example of speeches which are relatively difficult in content but which are delivered at a moderate pace that provides ample time for the mind to assimilate, understand and analyze them.

EXAMPLE: Statements by the United States in a case before the International Court of Justice.

Case: Certain Iranian Assets (Islamic Republic of Iran v. United States of America) – Public hearings on the Preliminary Objections raised by the United States.

https://www.icj-cij.org/en/multimedia/5bbb1ed5a12d880415cfb5cf

The rate at which speeches are delivered at international meetings has increased dramatically. While normal speech is uttered at an average rate of about 120–150 words per minute, it is not unusual nowadays to hear speeches delivered at a rate of 170 words per minute. Nor is it unusual for speeches delivered that fast to contain passages of extraordinary difficulty.

Under these conditions, how much semantic content should a competent conference interpreter be expected to render from the source language to the target language? Viewing the matter with an eye to quality, it seems fair to say that an interpreter should exercise sound editorial judgment in deciding what must be fully conveyed and what can be safely edited while keeping pace with the speaker and respecting the original meaning and intent, and should strive to convey all of the speaker's meaning even if it requires systematically condensing verbiage and abridging or deleting details that are obvious, redundant, or superfluous.

To strike the right balance between accuracy and completeness, i.e. to know what to edit or omit, requires the interpreter to be keenly aware of gradations in meaning and intent by the speaker, and to prioritize what she hears. A good starting point for this analysis is to observe that interpretation is sometimes imperfect but is so because it is a form of human speech, which is also imperfect. Some things that come from a speaker's mouth are merely disfluencies or noise ('er, ahem,' 'indeed,' etc.) and need not be treated as meaningful utterances. And it is known that, at a certain speed of delivery, distortions triggered by cognitive overload will cause some words not to be recognized. Nor is this due to any human failing or mental laziness on the part of the interpreter, since computerized speech recognition systems suffer from the same problem.

What is an interpreting error?

What is an interpreting error? Most such problems occur when an interpreter is forced to talk too fast. Inadvertent transpositions of sounds, such as 'spoonerisms' (confusing similar words, e.g. 'statements' and 'statesmen') are not interpreting errors, since they can occur within one and the same language in everyday speech.[127] The same can be said of common mispronunciations and malapropisms. And when an interpreter misuses language because the speaker has done so, the error is not the interpreter's (although most interpreters will try to correct such errors when they can). An interpreting error occurs when words properly used in the Source Language are improperly rendered in the Target Language in such a manner that the meaning conveyed is misleading to some or all members of the audience or the meaning is conveyed in the wrong tone or register. Sometimes, especially at expert meetings, an unfamiliar term misused by the interpreter will not mislead anyone and will merely cause a few smiles or furrowed brows. But it is an error when an interpreter says something substantially different from or contrary to what the speaker said, or omits a significant point, or renders the speaker's meaning in the wrong tone or register. It may be useful, therefore, to distinguish between trivial errors or *lapsus linguae* on the one hand and non-trivial or substantive errors on the other.

It sometimes happens that the combination of complexity, detail and speed will cause speaking errors or *lapsus linguae* in the original Source Language speech, such as inadvertent repetitions, stumbling, inappropriate pauses in mid-sentence, or slurred pronunciation of certain words. This often occurs when a speaker is nervous or is reading out a prepared speech and facing a time-limit. A court interpreter might allow such features of speech to show through but a conference interpreter will normally strive to minimize them in the Target Language.

How and when to correct substantive interpretation errors

Substantive interpreting errors, those which could affect the course of the discussion if they went unnoticed and unrectified, need to be corrected, and it is the interpreter's responsibility to admit his/her mistake and take whatever steps are necessary to avert or rectify misunderstandings. This is best done at the end of an exchange or meeting by bringing the error to the attention of the speaker, the presiding officer and/or the record-writers. If the course of the discussion has been affected by an interpreting error, the correction should be made as soon as possible. On the other hand, interpreters should avoid creating unnecessary distraction by apologizing on the microphone for a trivial error or slip of the tongue.

Using generality to avoid misleading error

One of the most misleading errors an interpreter can make is a complete omission, since it tends to go unnoticed and gives the listener no clue about what the speaker said. An omitted sentence containing an important logical link can muddle the meaning of what came before it and what comes after it as well. Consequently, it is better not to be a perfectionist and to give the listener a reasonably good idea of what the speaker has said even if it is not perfectly accurate or complete. In interpreting you will sometimes hear a word or phrase that you understand partly but not fully, or which you can translate partly but not fully. The option of dropping the entire phrase is not the best option and should be a last resort. A better solution is to rephrase the utterance in more general terms. For example, if the speaker says 'Il faut protéger les espèces amazoniennes les plus vulnérables tels les primates lémuriens,' it is better to say 'We must protect the most vulnerable Amazon species' than to say nothing because you are baffled about how to translate 'primates lémuriens.'

6 Protocol and Etiquette of Interpreting

The following suggestions are addressed to more advanced interpreting students and practitioners, as well as to meeting planners and consulting interpreters.

Use consecutive interpretation when appropriate or when required

Situations arise in which it is impractical to provide and set up simultaneous interpretation equipment, e.g. urgent meetings held on short notice, impromptu interviews, breakout group meetings held in small rooms, confidential one-on-one negotiations, press conferences held outdoors, confidential medical or psychiatric evaluations, interrogations. For such situations, consecutive interpretation is still the norm. Interpretation for short meetings (under one hour) can sometimes be done by a single interpreter, and it is thought by some that the use of a single interpreter rather than a team enhances confidentiality. Consecutive is also used by most court systems at trials and hearings, and by lawyers for depositions. It requires little or no equipment and has the additional advantage of providing brief pauses during which the participants can think about what has been said and mull over their next question or statement. Performing consecutive interpretation, whether in training or on the job, helps interpreters to develop skills that are also useful in simultaneous interpretation.

Situations also arise in diplomatic intercourse where several languages are being used in a complex or delicate negotiation but consecutive is used in preference to the faster simultaneous method because the parties involved want to take the extra time and/or because the stakes are so high that they only trust their own interpreters, making it necessary for the conversation to proceed step by step, with the parties taking the floor in turn and the interpretation(s) being spoken between speeches or during pauses.

A GROWING DIPLOMATIC AGENDA – [Zhang Lu] said her duties had become busier as China had expanded its diplomatic agenda in recent years. The year 2015 was her busiest ever, with her making 54 overseas trips with Chinese leaders.

'The fact you work for the state leaders... [means] when you speak, when you interpret, people will not only take your words as the individual's voice, but also as the voice of authority,' she said.

Zhang's most memorable experience was as a translator at the Six-party talks aiming to find a peaceful resolution to Pyongyang's nuclear weapons programme, involving China, the United States, Japan, Russia, South Korea and North Korea, between 2003 to 2008.

'It involved very interesting and challenging diplomatic negotiations,' she said.

Because of the sensitivity of the issue, the language used by each participating nation was regarded as the official language of the talks, so **each delegation brought their own interpreters**.

She said every time the head of a nation's delegation paused while making a speech, all the interpreters of different countries immediately began interpreting at the same time.

'So you can imagine ... how long it took for one person to finish a single sentence' she said.

In her own words: translator to China's top leaders takes centre stage in Hong Kong. South China Morning Post, 9 April 2016. (excerpt). Reproduced by permission of South China Morning Post.

[http://www.scmp.com/news/china/policies-politics/article/1934922/her-own-words-translator-chinas-top-leaders-takes]

Develop a personal note-taking system based on your own handwriting

Many people nowadays have formed the habit of taking notes on their laptop computers, which may be an efficient way of keeping track of material presented in some meetings or lectures but is not a good method to use for consecutive interpretation because it does not encourage immediate analysis of the material, since most of one's mental and physical effort is taken up by merely capturing the material. Handwritten notes are more conducive to 'thinking your way through' the material. See, for example, the results of a recent study:

Generative note-taking

Mueller and Oppenheimer cited that note-taking can be categorized two ways: generative and nongenerative. Generative note-taking pertains to 'summarizing, paraphrasing, concept mapping,' while nongenerative note-taking involves copying something verbatim. And there are two hypotheses as to why note-taking is beneficial in the first place. The first idea is called the encoding hypothesis, which says that when a person is taking notes, 'the processing that occurs' will improve 'learning and retention.' The second, called the external-storage hypothesis, is that you learn by being able to look back at your notes, or even the notes of other people.

Because people can type faster than they write, using a laptop will make people more likely to try to transcribe everything they're hearing. So on the one hand, Mueller and Oppenheimer were faced with the question of whether the benefits of being able to look at your more complete, transcribed notes on a laptop outweigh the drawbacks of not processing that information. On the other hand, when writing longhand, you process the information better but have less to look back at.

Attention, Students: Put Your Laptops Away, NPR, 17 April 2016 (excerpt)

http://www.npr.org/2016/04/17/474525392/attention-students-put-your-laptops-away?utm_source=npr_newsletter&utm_medium=email&utm_content=20160424&utm_campaign=bestofnpr&utm_term=nprnews

---

Interpreter notes. Photo by author.

Interrupt the speaker as little as possible but as often as necessary to get it right

When performing consecutive interpretation, be courteous but don't be timid. You cannot afford to let the speaker race ahead of you so far that you will be unable to render what he said or to catch up with him before he finishes. You must be brave enough to step forward and begin interpreting when your memory and note-taking skill are reaching their limits, even if it means interrupting the speaker. Otherwise, you will end up committing errors and omissions, which is a disservice to the speaker.

If the speaker pauses, use those pauses to interpret

Usually, the most unobtrusive way to provide consecutive interpretation is to try to avoid interrupting the speaker by inserting interpreted segments into the pauses taken by the speaker himself. However, one must be careful not to let the speaker go on so long that the interpreter's short-term memory is strained beyond its limits, because then it may become necessary to ask the speaker to repeat, which wastes his time rather than saving it.

The following recorded press encounter contains several short speeches with pre-scripted pauses and some pre-translated interpretations. The style of delivery is unhurried and ceremonial. Play back the video, pause it to insert your own interpretations, and compare your renditions with those of the interpreters who performed at the event.

https://www.youtube.com/watch?v=URKeYhpZuZc

Pre-arrange the pace of interruptions if possible: Agree on a cue

Be realistic about your own abilities. If you know that you have never been able to do consecutive interpretation accurately for more than 3 minutes at a time, then ask the speaker to let you interpret the speech in 3-minute segments. If the speaker agrees to this, then agree with the speaker on a cue he can use to let you know when to begin your next interpreting segment. For example, ask the speaker to turn and nod to you, or to raise his hand, when he wants you to begin interpreting. Such a prearranged cue can prevent the kind of problem mentioned at the end of the 'Zhang-Lu' example above ('She said every time the head of a nation's delegation paused while making a speech, all the interpreters of different countries immediately began interpreting at the same time. So you can imagine … how long it took for one person to finish a single sentence she said.') As you gain experience, you will be able to lengthen your interpretation segments, and eventually to do 'long consecutive', interpreting a whole speech from beginning to end, using notes to help your memory.

If possible, use condensation to keep your consecutive interpretation segments short

While giving your consecutive interpretation it is important to 'keep moving'. No audience likes to be kept waiting. There is no point in dwelling on a difficulty or error. More importantly, the slower you go and the more you pause, the more information you are losing because short-term memory fades very rapidly and you will soon reach a point where the notes you took no longer make sense to you. So keep up the momentum even if it means you have to resort to condensing some parts of the speech.

Ask for repetition if you have missed an important point

If you have not fully understood or cannot fully render a point which you sense may be important, it is better to avoid omission and ask the speaker to repeat or to clarify. This should not be difficult or embarrassing if you have been doing a good job and have a good rapport with the speaker. Most speakers will gladly help, and the interpreter's sincerity is appreciated.

Stand or sit to one side of, and slightly behind, the speaker; step forward to interpret, then step back

Your position in relation to the speakers is dictated by two consider-ations: you need to be close enough to hear everything the speakers say but not so close that you upstage or distract the speakers. If the acoustics of the room require amplification of voices by a public address system and you do not have your own microphone, you may need to share the micro-phone the speaker is using in order to be heard by others, so you will have to stand relatively near the speaker.[128] Stand to one side of, and slightly behind, the speaker; step or lean forward, then move back. This small movement will set up a routine that makes it easier for you to intervene throughout the speech to give your interpretation segments. If the micro-phone you are sharing with a speaker is a portable one, be careful not to drop it or strike a surface with it, since the noise it makes can be deafening and disruptive.

Be discreet and unobtrusive; avoid distracting attention from the speaker

Some speakers do not like to have an interpreter standing next to them because they feel that the interpreter 'steals the show', breaks their train of thought or hampers their direct rapport with the audience. They see the interpreter as a 'necessary evil'. Try to minimize this problem by making

Drawing by 'Clic' – Benoît CLIQUET. 'Interpreters – the drawings'. aiic.net October 25, 2004. Reproduced by permission of the artist.

your presence as discreet and unobtrusive as possible. Take care with your appearance and demeanor.

In a dialogue or joint news conference, stand or sit between the speakers

In a dialogue or joint news event, be sure to make arrangements before the event begins to be positioned between the two parties. If they are seated facing each other and you are placed next to one of them, you may end up having to raise your voice in order to be heard by the other, which is distracting to them and creates an undesirable appearance of bias. By taking your place between them you are showing your impartiality as an interpreter.

For *chuchotage*, stand or sit next to or (if necessary) behind the client

Chuchotage is whispered simultaneous/consecutive interpretation. It is usually performed for one or two people who do not understand the language being used by others at the meeting. The physical location of the interpreter is important because she must be able to hear everything that is being said around her but be close enough to the client so that the client can hear her whispering but others in the room are not disturbed by it. If the meeting audio is being broadcast through earphone receivers, be sure to request one for yourself. That may be the only way you can hear a speaker at the opposite end of the table from you.

Whispering. Reproduced courtesy of Milega Translations

In a group setting, stay close to the keynote speaker

When interpreting in a group setting, stand or sit as close as possible to the keynote speaker so that you can hear everything he or she says. Agree beforehand with the participants on how much involvement is expected of you, i.e. whose interventions you are to interpret, and for whose benefit. In the situation shown below, the author was acting as a standby interpreter for the Spanish film director Pedro Almodovar and intervened only to the extent that Mr. Almodovar needed help to express himself in English.

Interpreting for Pedro Almodovar on the Charlie Rose Show. Photo by author.

When interpreting a group interaction, position yourself at the center of the action so that you can hear and be heard by all participants

Interpreting at a hearing of the International Tribunal for the Law of the Sea (*Camouco case*). Photo by author.

When podiums or tables are being used, ask for a seat or a surface on which to write, in order to facilitate note-taking

When interpreting an exchange between seated interlocutors, ask to be seated on a level with them if possible. It is harder to hear them and to take good notes while standing or stooping.

When the interlocutors are on the move, be prepared to follow and keep up

Pope Francis talking and walking with President Barack Obama. Interpreter: Monsignor Mark Miles. Drawing by Jamie Nolan. Reproduced by permission of the artist.

Interpreted meeting while touring between President Putin and Prime Minister Modi. Reproduced by permission of the photographer, Dr. Vipin Kumar.

Being positioned between the speakers is as important when the parties are walking as when they are seated, since walking along beside one of them can make it hard to hear or be heard by the other, depending on the volume of their voices. An interpreter need not be shy about asking interlocutors to speak up so that he can hear them properly, or asking them to slow down if they are walking too fast for him to follow the exchange.

Height, posture and body language play a role in this type of situation: '...the fact that he appears to be a whole head shorter than the 78-year-old pontiff (though that may be just a posture issue, since he's always leaning into the conversation). It might be the way he moves his hands like a conductor, how he gestures to the people he's interpreting, and how the pope often responds with his own gestures, so that the pair seems on always on the verge of a low five, or a secret handshake.' [Dan Zak, 'Meet Monsignor Mark Miles,' Washington Post, 25 September 2015.]

Use gestures moderately

Although we usually think of gestures as an aid to speech used to emphasize or punctuate what we are saying, gesturing is actually 'an ancient trait that precedes the existence of modern humans and of language.'[129] Gesturing occurs commonly and spontaneously, and interpreters need not try to suppress it out of an excessive sense of decorum. Speakers may use gestures to convey a significant part of the message, especially the emotive part. It is generally not necessary for an interpreter to mirror or 'mimic' gestures: if the interpreter is working in a booth, he is not visible to the audience; and if he is doing consecutive standing next to the speaker, the speaker's own gesture is enough. If gesturing helps you to capture and reflect the content and intent of the speaker, or helps you to release tension, by all means do so, but use moderate, measured gestures if you are working in front of an audience. Remember also that if a speaker expresses an idea or nuance by gesturing but you cannot do the same because you are in the confined space of a booth or you cannot be seen because your booth is at the back of the hall, you still have the alternative of expressing the gestural nuance or emphasis with your voice. And remember that if you can see the speakers from the booth, it is wise to always keep an eye on the person speaking because it can happen that a gesture will transform the meaning of a verbal utterance or even replace an utterance (e.g. shrugging the shoulders can mean 'I don't know', upward pointing of the thumbs can mean 'I approve', etc.). Naturally, if you are interpreting from a spoken language into signed language, the target-language gestures you use may be different from the gestures used by the speaker. Also, be aware that in some languages certain gestures are taboo. And if an inexperienced speaker's body language is actually a form of involuntary nervous fidgeting, such as drumming his fingers on the table out of impatience or scratching his head in puzzlement, you should not try to copy such movements, since doing so may attract too much attention to them and appear to be a kind of parody.

UN DPI Photo 737165 – Sim Abdoulaye Diop, Minister of Foreign Affairs of Mali speaking to Security Council, as seen from the viewpoint of an interpreter in the Arabic booth – Photo by Kim Haughton, taken 5 October 2017. Reproduced by permission.

Verbal and gestural denotation are interrelated, and accompanying what we say by relevant gestures of hand symbols is second nature, a sub-conscious process. Orators presenting to an audience have always used gestures for emphasis, i.e. to give added power or emotive persuasiveness to some the words they use. If an interpreter cannot fully portray a gesture visually from the concealment of a booth, she/he should attempt to convey the nuance by voice. This video illustrates how manual gesturing can help the interpreter to structure the verbal message she is producing:

https://www.facebook.com/aurora.humaran/posts/2996159310446404?comment_id=3000861189976216&reply_comment_id=3001999779862357

Empedocles.

Ancient Greek philosopher Empedocles gesturing. New York Public Library Digital Collections. Public domain image 1624771. https://digitalcollections.nypl.org/items/510d47e4-476d-a3d9-e040-e00a18064a99

Gestures can also be used to magnify an emotion or to illustrate the intensity or complexity of a thought or utterance by imparting a given shape to the arm, hand or fingers. If there is unintended vagueness or ambiguity in the words used by a speaker, gestures sometimes clarify the intended meaning and an interpreter may then have the option of also clarifying it for his listeners. Sign language interpreters, using both hand signs and facial expressions, are skilled at visually expressing messages of great subtlety and complexity.

Billy Rose Theatre Division, The New York Public Library Digital Collections. (1963). Actor George C. Scott gesturing with finger Retrieved from http://digitalcollections. nypl.org/items/ccf434f0-753b-0130-17bd-58d385a7bbd0, New York Public Library public domain image 1624771.

Thelma Kotze and Asanda Katshwa (foreground) SASL interpreters, at James Nolan seminar, WITS, Johannesburg, 2010

The story of Lydia Callis – 'A Bright Light During Dark Days: Bloomberg's Sign Language Star' (excerpts)

Since we noted Monday that the sign language interpreter for New York City Mayor Michael Bloomberg (I) was becoming an Internet sensation, her fan base seems to have kept on growing.

Identified by the mayor as Lydia Callis, her expressive style has fascinated many and provided a bit of a bright light amid all the dark news about Superstorm Sandy. As New York magazine says, she's given 'New Yorkers a legitimate reason to smile' during some very hard times.

Now, as happens these days, there's a Tumblr page – Lydia Callis's Face For NYC Mayor – and the discussion about her continues on Twitter.

If you haven't seen what folks are finding fascinating, there's a video here.'

[Excerpt from NPR: http://www.npr.org/blogs/thetwo-way/ 2012/10/30/163940098/a-bright-light-during-dark-news-bloombergs-sign-language-star]

'In the wake of superstorm Sandy this week, several unlikely stars have stepped into the spotlight. Among them? **Lydia Callis**, New York City Mayor Michael Bloomberg's awesomely animated sign language interpreter, whose expressive translations at recent press conferences have been compared to first-class performance art.

She's media shy. Unlike other overnight stars, Callis doesn't appear eager to extend her 15 minutes of fame. After declining to be interviewed by Bloomberg Businessweek after a recent press conference, she told the *New York Post*, 'I'm here to serve the deaf and hard-of-hearing community. I'm just glad, and I'm honored, that I was able to get the message out there...that's what it's all about.' As Rochester's Livadas explained, 'By nature, the role of an interpreter is to accommodate effective communication, not to be the story. She may be uncomfortable with all the hype.'

She's skilled at improv. Though the **Post** reports that Callis <u>watches the news to anticipate and account for potentially challenging concepts</u> – like the words 'surge' and 'crane' – she doesn't get the mayor's speeches in advance and has to think quickly on her feet. That means being ready for anything – including Bloomberg's unpredictable behavior. 'If he stutters, if he messes up a sentence, you're going to see me stuttering, and you're going to see me messing up the sentence,' she told DNAinfo, adding that she also <u>tries to convey his sometimes-sarcastic tone through facial expressions.</u> 'The point of interpreting is to render the message faithfully, and that's what I have to do.' [emphasis added]

[Excerpt from US News: http://www.usmagazine.com/celebrity-news/ news/mayor-bloombergs-sign-language-interpreter-lydia-callis-5-things -you-dont-know-20123110]

[See also: UN Website celebrating International Day of Sign Languages:
https://www.facebook.com/unitednations/videos/558856091216300/ UzpfSTIzMjEwMTc5NzYyMzY0ODoyODM3NTE1ODU3OTIwMDI/]

When interpreting prepared speeches, use sight translation rather than notes as your aide-mémoire

Prepared speeches are usually read out at faster-than-normal speed, which makes note taking more difficult and less reliable. If you learn that the speaker plans to read out a long prepared speech, immediately approach him or his delegation and ask for a copy. If he only has scribbled notes or talking points, ask to borrow it and go to the nearest photocopy machine and make a copy for yourself. When doing consecutive, it will usually be more effective to do a sight translation from the prepared speech than to rely mainly on notes. As the speech is being delivered, you can mentally prepare your translation and add annotations and marginal notes to the text that will help you to correctly render and to abridge it during delivery. When doing simultaneous, the text will help you to avoid omissions and to correctly render titles, names, acronyms, statistics, dates, etc. If you are given your copy in advance of delivery, you may even have time to analyze and pre-translate some difficult words or phrases, so that during your rendition you will be able to concentrate more on style.

Explain professional standards and technical requirements to the client

Some interpretation clients you encounter in the course of your work may not be familiar with the technical and professional practices, rules and standards followed by interpreters. It is part of your job to explain them, answer questions about them and clarify the reasons for them. A key area of concern, particularly for police, judicial, military and diplomatic clients, is confidentiality.[130] You should make clear to your clients that everything you hear in the course of an interpretation assignment will be treated as strictly confidential and that any notes you take are used only to help your memory during the assignment, are legible only to you, and may be destroyed or turned over to the client at the end of the assignment if they so request. It is important to make clear to clients that they can trust you and that you observe confidentiality as a matter of principle and as a professional obligation, in the same manner as a doctor, lawyer or priest. Otherwise, some clients concerned about confidentiality may try to burden you with cumbersome protocols, restrictions or technologies that they see as important to safeguard their privacy but which may prevent you from doing a good job. For example, the author once accepted an assignment to interpret for a meeting of the Board of Directors of a large New York bank only to discover that the interpreting booths they had set up did not have windows because they did not want the interpreters to know the identities of the board members, fearing that something might be 'leaked' to the news media. The two interpreters were also asked to share only one headset in order to minimize the amount of information being disclosed by allowing only interpreter at a time to hear only what was strictly necessary to interpret the person who was currently speaking. Being deprived of a view of the speakers in the board room and being denied the ability to follow the whole thread of the discussions made the interpreters' work much more difficult and made it impossible for them to work as a team.

Similar problems may arise when conference organizers use portable (collapsible) tabletop interpreting booths. These booths may only partially block the ambient conference room noise. Depending on design, they may have windows too small to permit adequate visibility. Or they may allow only a reduced view of the speaker displayed on a tabletop monitor. The author once worked at a conference where, due to the insufficient soundproofing of the tabletop booth, the booth had to be moved midway through the meeting and placed in a doorway so that the interpreters could sit in an adjoining room and be less exposed to extraneous noise.

When interpreting for the media, be clear about your requirements

When interpreting for radio, television and internet broadcasters, especially if the program will be broadcast live, you must be very specific and insistent about your requirements. Doing so may cause producers or technicians to perceive you as being 'high maintenance' but the fact remains that when something goes wrong for technical reasons, the media will often proclaim to the world that it was 'the fault of the interpretation'. When working for a broadcaster, you are usually placed either in front of a monitor in the studio or on a sound stage with other people. Unless the producer is familiar with how interpreters work, you may find at the last minute (when it is too late to do anything about it) that the picture or sound quality you are receiving through your monitor and headset are too faint or too distorted for you to interpret correctly. Or, if you are on a sound stage as part of an interview or panel discussion, you may find at the last minute (when it is too late to do anything about it) that you are hearing through your earphones not just the speaker you are interpreting but also everybody else present, including yourself! (Because that is what all other people on a sound stage normally hear through their earphones, and no one has bothered to tell the sound engineer about the specific requirement of the interpreter.) So be prepared, be specific about what you need in order to do a good job, and don't be shy about educating the producer or sound engineer. If the sound system in use is one that has been prone to generating noises or spikes in volume that can be damaging to interpreters' hearing, approach the conference organizer or the AV provider before you begin work and ask to be provided with compressor limiters as a safeguard against acoustic shock.

For a helpful introduction to broadcast interpreting and related technical practices and journalistic constraints, see the lecture given by Professor Chikako Tsuruta at the University of Hawaii:

https://www.youtube.com/watch?v=i7028hDWM3A
https://www.youtube.com/watch?v=-qS_U0fznL0

For some good examples of broadcast interpreting, see the following:

Barack Obama: https://www.youtube.com/watch?v=KcrbmGsf1KY
Tim Kaine: https://www.youtube.com/watch?v=nfuEwESqSW4
Michael Bloomberg: https://www.youtube.com/watch?v=YLTrDaFUVg8
François Hollande: https://www.youtube.com/watch?v=mmoY7G_6MgQ

For a discussion of interpreting for broadcast sporting events, see:

https://www.planetfootball.com/in-depth/the-story-of-the-uefa-translator-who-went-viral-thanks-to-jurgen-klopp/

When working in a booth, be orderly and keep the documents well organized and within easy reach so that you can find the right one quickly

Author interpreting at UN. Photo by author.

Obtaining copies of the main conference documents (agenda, speakers' list) before the conference begins and studying them is highly recommended. Once you are in the booth, it is also very useful to be able to quickly find the right document in the target language and read out from it passages that the speaker is reading out verbatim in the source language, sometimes very fast. This not only saves mental energy but also enables you to produce preferred or conventional wordings that the audience expects to hear. In a drafting group, don't try to re-invent the wheel by coming up with what you think is a better version of a provision under discussion; if a target-language version of that provision is already in the documents, it may be the product of many hours of debate and negotiation, and your spontaneous attempt to improve upon it may be counterproductive and cause delay.

Webcast events

Webcast events often involve multiple feeds. It is important that the interpreters receive the actual sound broadcast over the original language channel. Technicians should test all feeds well in advance of the event to work out any issues or 'bugs' before the event begins. A multilingual webcast is a live recording of simultaneous interpreting. It is not intended to be a literal or definitive translation of the proceedings. Further, webcasting of simultaneous interpretation may be subject to copyright. This requires the interpreters' prior consent and may call for additional payment.

Consider the visibility and lines of sight in the conference room

Interpreters need to see the speakers they are interpreting and to be aware of what is happening at the meeting, e.g. who is in attendance, an important person's arrival or departure, someone gesturing to make a point of order, the result of a vote being shown on an electronic voting display in the conference room, a piece of demonstrative evidence being shown in the courtroom, etc. However, architects are increasingly designing interpretation booths placed high above the floor of the conference room, and they do not always make provision for monitors to enable the interpreters to see speakers through a closed-circuit camera system, or large screens in the conference room displaying an enlarged picture of the speaker. If you normally need glasses in order to see clearly at a distance, be sure not to forget them.

Ensure that conference documents will be provided

If the documents are important to understanding and interpreting the proceedings or to correctly hearing and pronouncing the names and titles of participants, be sure that a way has been arranged to get copies of the documents to the interpreters in time for them to be of use. It is best for that task to be assigned to a conference-room usher or documents clerk, since the interpreters need to be in their booths following the proceedings from the start. But, if necessary, an interpreter should be willing to do this himself, provided the language combinations in use allow one member of the team to be absent briefly from the booth without a lapse in coverage. If it seems unlikely that the client will provide conference documents, retrieve as much background material as you can from the internet, print it out, and bring it with you. Sometimes, the documentation for a meeting may be available online and accessible from your laptop computer, so it is generally wise to have your laptop with you and to arrange internet access.

Request monitors with a closed-circuit video view of speakers when necessary

In some large conference spaces, the placement of the booths may be such that a direct view of the speakers through the booth window is impossible or inadequate, e.g. when the booth is too far from the speakers, too high above the conference room floor, or positioned so that one sees only the speakers' backs. For some large conferences with multiple languages, the only place where the booths can be placed may be at the back of the hall (see picture). When conference speakers are seated in a circular layout, about one half of their faces will not be visible to the interpreters regardless of where the booths are placed (see pictures). In such cases, it is advisable to ask that a better view of the speakers be provided by means of monitors connected to closed-circuit video cameras. At most meetings, speakers generally take the floor one at a time and speak from the rostrum, so that it is necessary to set up only one video camera focused on the rostrum.

Booths positioned on a stage at a conference. Photo by Acielle Zelenina. Reproduced by permission.

Advice on placement of booths – from Calliope-Interpreters

Reproduced with kind permission of Calliope-Interpreters.

Interpreters usually work in fixed or mobile booths placed in the room where the conference is taking place. They must be able to hear the speakers perfectly and observe the non-verbal signals that characterize communication; to see the projection screens displaying presentations or other information; and be able to ensure, by directly observing the people listening, that the message they have translated has been successfully conveyed.

Replicating those conditions in a remote situation is complex. First and foremost, it is crucial that the audio and video link between the meeting room and the interpreters is achieved by means of an internal, physical cable. In addition, to preserve the quality of the interpretation service provided, Calliope-Interpreters makes the following recommendations:

Choose a quiet location for the interpretation booths, preferably an adjacent room.

Inform the cameramen and sound technicians about the interpreters' needs.

Ensure that, despite not being in the same room as the delegates, the interpreters receive the same information as them.

Ensure that technicians are specifically assigned to the interpretation, both in the meeting room and with the interpreters, to ensure that the microphones are being used properly, that the sound transmitted is of the necessary quality, and that the sound-image synchronization is perfect.

The audio link must comply with ISO 20109:2016, which provides for a faithful reproduction of frequencies between 125Hz and 15,000Hz across the entire speaker-interpreter-audience system so that the message can be comfortably understood and none of its content is lost.

To ensure that the interpreters have a clear view of the speakers, audience and projection screen, each booth should be equipped with two high-resolution, sufficiently large, colour monitors showing

- on the first monitor, the presenter, and if appropriate, the chairman of the meeting and the rostrum, or the various panel members in the case of a roundtable discussion or question-and-answer session, as well as any speakers from the audience;
- on the second monitor, the content being screened. If the content is being projected from a computer, a direct feed between the computer in the room and the interpreters' monitors should be provided, as this will give a crisper image.

The monitors should be placed at eye level, preferably outside and directly in front of the booths.

Clearly, the ideal scenario is to have interpreters in the meeting room with the delegates. However, if space constraints require the interpretation booths to be removed, remote interpreting can be a practical solution, in particular when the interpreters remain in the same building as the delegates, and both sound and images are supplied by means of a physical cable. The above guidelines will ensure that the conference is a success despite the interpreters being in a (slightly) remote location.[131]

Speaker at podium is sufficiently visible from back rows, thanks to screen. (World Conservation Congress, press conference, September 2016). Photo by author.

Large screens can be used in conference rooms to display enlarged picture(s) of the speaker(s) visible from the interpretation booths. (World Conservation Congress, press conference, September 2016). Photo by author.

The interpreter can sometimes retrieve from the internet useful background information about a speaker or about the subject of a speech, or even a closeup view of the speaker if the meeting is being webcast. IUCN World Conservation Congress, September 2016. Photo by author.

If the screen is too far from the booth, displays such as power-point texts may not be legible to the interpreters. They should be supplemented by a monitor in the booth or hard-copy versions of the documents. (IUCN World Conservation Congress, September 2016) Photo by author

Observe professional ethics and encourage compliance with standards

In your professional activity, you should observe the ethical rules and standards contained in the code of the International Association of Conference Interpreters (AIIC) or, *mutatis mutandis*, other such codes that may apply to you. You need to be able to clarify such rules and standards to your clients and explain the reasons for them. In addition, courts and tribunals may also require you to observe certain protocols, sign a pledge of confidentiality or take an oath. At the national level, you should encourage conference sponsors and organizers to comply with established standards such as the ASTM Standard Guide for Language Interpretation Services (F 2089-01).[132]

Maintain and enhance your skills and marketability through continuing education and training

In the world of interpreting, standing still may mean falling behind. The relative importance of languages changes rapidly with changes in the political and demographic landscape. For example, at this writing, in 2018, there is increasing use of German and French in the EU institutions in Brussels due to the announced withdrawal of the UK, while at the same time the importance of English as a 'bridge' language or lingua franca is maintained. Globally, Mandarin is rapidly overtaking English as the major international language. It is essential to maintain your language knowledge and interpreting skills through regular practice, whether on the job or on your own, and to keep abreast of trends in your working languages through exposure in person by travel or vicariously

Spanish A > English B
James Nolan conference interpreting seminar
Frankfurt, Germany, 2010. Photo by author.

English ◇ Spanish
James Nolan skill-building seminar for court interpreters
Idaho Supreme Court & Ada County District Court Boise, Idaho, 2009. Photo by author.

via the media and the internet. It is also helpful to attend subject-matter lectures or workshops on your areas of specialization. Nowadays, there are many opportunities for interpreters to obtain continuing education and training that can enable you to maintain or expand your language combination, for example by turning a passive 'C' language into a 'B' language which may enable you to take advantage of wider opportunities in your local market. Sometimes, institutional employers such as court systems may offer support or subsidies for continuing-education workshops to help regularly employed interpreters keep up the quality of their services.

7 Situations: Ethical and Practical Considerations

Seen as a multicultural code embodying the means to channel communications and to enable dispute resolution between various nations and cultures that use differing codes, translation / interpretation often plunges its practitioners into realms of ambiguity and conflict. And yet, it is a testament to the maturity attained by the profession that a contemporary interpreter's life is, for the most part, quite stable and uneventful. The most serious problem of ethics, public relations or crisis-management that most interpreters will ever have to deal with is the occasional speaker who feels that an interpreter's rendition has not done justice to his or her remarks, which can usually be resolved by an apology. However, when quick decisions have to be made in the course of a meeting about matters of sound practice and ethics, they should not be 'snap' decisions but rather decisions based on mature prior consideration and an understanding of the issues. The situations presented here are meant to encourage readers to engage in that reflection.

These situations are not all typical. Rather, they were singled out to illustrate and dramatize some of the practical and ethical problems translators and interpreters may encounter, in less acute form, in their day-to-day work, using the benefit of hindsight and the perspective that history and distance can provide.

1 The Value of Interpreting

Cultural perceptions about the value of translation and interpretation vary widely. Interpretation tends to be perceived as a more valuable or prestigious occupation in multilingual societies. Consider the following recollection by President Nelson Mandela of South Africa:

> Although K.D. was counselling me to study law, I had my heart set on being an interpreter or clerk in the Native Affairs Department. At that time, a career as a civil servant was a glittering prize for an African, the highest that a black man could aspire to. In the rural

areas, an interpreter in the magistrate's office was considered second only in importance to the magistrate himself. When, in my second year, Fort Hare introduced an interpreting course taught by a distinguished retired court interpreter, Tyamzashe, I was one of the first students to sign up. [Nelson Mandela, Long Walk to Freedom]

The situation in South Africa today has evolved markedly since the days when Dugmore Boetie wrote the following description of how interpreters were employed under apartheid in the context of 'Influx Control,' a public agency serving to enforce mandatory employment rules for Africans. The organization of this agency reflected the subordinate status of the native languages that the interpreters were there to translate. That subordinate status was also reflected in the fact that the communication was not regarded as a sufficient job in itself and the interpreters were required to perform additional ancillary functions, including aiding in the enforcement of oppressive regulations, a problem which also arises today in the context of immigration and border-crossing situations and when interpreting is farmed out to 'one-stop-shop' agencies that undervalue the interpreting service or combine it with logistical services and expect the interpreters they hire to do double duty by also performing clerical or menial tasks.

Inside was a hall with a giant horseshoe-shaped counter. Behind the counter were divided cubicles. In each cubicle sat a white clerk. On the hall side, opposite each cubicle, were barroom stools where black interpreters sat. An iron grille divided the interpreters from the white clerks. Nowhere in this vast arena was there a place where the job-seekers could sit. ...

The interpreter would hand your pass through the grille to the white clerk who would take his time studying it. If there was an irregularity, he'd give it back to the interpreter with instructions.

The interpreter would hang on to your pass which you didn't dare leave without. He'd then shout, 'Escort!' Two police would appear and escort you upstairs to the interrogation room.[133]

2 Motives for Using Interpretation

Parties to a negotiation sometimes use 'the language barrier' as a diplomatic ploy in a variety of ways: to block the negotiating process, to slow it down, to stall for time while refining a proposal or consulting with their principals, to back away from an extreme position when they have gone too far ('I didn't say that; the interpreter did'), etc.

It is part of a diplomatic interpreter's job to take such things in stride and help the parties to communicate with each other, but only to the extent that they <u>want</u> to communicate. The interpreter, in other words, is not per se a multilingual mediator. He or she does not intervene in the process or take unsolicited initiatives to 'break the ice'. Otherwise, the interpreter would be jeopardizing his or her neutrality. However, it is common for official employers to try to save money by using an interpreter both for interpretation and to perform some other related diplomatic, administrative or political task. Sometimes, parties may ask an interpreter to perform certain functions simply because the interpreter is already at the scene or is seen as a neutral third party who has no stake in the outcome of the dispute and whom they can both trust. Consider the following:

In 1191, King Richard the Lionheart of England was attempting to recapture Jerusalem from the Moslems. His military campaign stalled, he tried to arrange a meeting with Saladin, presumably to try to achieve by negotiation what he could not achieve on the battlefield. Saladin replied to King Richard's invitation as follows:

> Kings meet only after the conclusion of an accord. In any event, I do not understand your language, and you are ignorant of mine, and **we therefore need a translator** in whom we both have confidence. Let this man, then, act as a messenger between us. When we arrive at an understanding, we will meet, and friendship will prevail between us.[134]

Saladin was apparently temporizing in order to consolidate his gains and also probably because he did not trust King Richard, who had attempted to achieve his aims by ruse. The positions remained deadlocked, King Richard never managed to meet with Saladin, and Saladin kept control over Jerusalem and the other lands he had reconquered from the crusaders. King Richard eventually gave up and went back to England.

Thus, in this case, Saladin seems to have successfully played the language card as a diplomatic ploy to gain time[135] when delay could work to his advantage. Notice, however, that, even while using 'the language barrier' as a pretext to maintain the status quo, Saladin's message acknowledged in principle the need for the parties to be able to rely on a trustworthy translator, one 'in whom we both have confidence', if they had used one.

Notice also that, in Saladin's view, part of the translator's function would have been to help the parties keep their distance. As he saw it, the principals would not even have had to meet with each other face to face until some understanding had already been reached between them, using the translator as the channel of communication.

This latter element of the interpreter's work, providing 'diplomatic distance', remains present even today, when swift electronic media and the widespread availability of simultaneous interpretation have made 'the language barrier' a rather poor excuse for not communicating. When interpretation is provided, neither party has to condescend to speak the other's language, so that neither appears to be making concessions to the other's culture, which puts the two sides to a negotiation on a more equal footing. Arguably, this gives negotiations a better chance of getting off the ground, and also makes the end results more viable, since neither side will feel that the negotiation put them at a disadvantage by forcing them to use an unfamiliar language.

3 Role of the Interpreter

Ideally, a good interpreter blends in and becomes 'invisible': he or she helps the parties to understand each other almost as well as if they were speaking the same language. When interpretation arrangements have been properly made, it is rare to hear anyone during a meeting refer to the interpreters or to the fact that the proceedings are being interpreted. The participants simply go into the meeting and begin speaking in their own languages.

When parties to a dispute meet to talk it is assumed that they are aiming at some resolution. But what if the parties do not really <u>want</u> to understand each other and decide to use 'the language barrier' as a pretext, or as a weapon? Is such an impasse the interpreter's fault? Should the interpreter accept responsibility for a breakdown in communication? Consider the following stressful situation, which occurred during the break-up of the Yugoslav federation:

Dragoljub Micunovic, the leader of the Democratic Party from Serbia, was the conference host. He and his party had expended considerable effort bringing together so much mutual loathing around a single oval table in such a civilized manner. The intention of the participants was to achieve what the leaders of the six republics had failed to do so abysmally: to unearth the road to peace. Micunovic made this plain in a tactful and encouraging opening speech. He finished by saying that simultaneous translation of the proceedings into Slovene and Macedonian would be provided. This harmless remark was the signal for the remaining guests to inject a lethal dose of Balkan absurdity into the proceedings which would demolish any marginal hopes that the conference might have produced anything of value.

Neven Jurica, the leader of the Croatian Democratic Union (HDZ) delegation and an uncompromising Croat nationalist, raised his hand on a point of order. 'I was pleased to hear that Slovene and Macedonians translation will be provided but there are other languages as well to be translated. What about our Hungarian and Albanian colleagues?' A fair enough question, to which Micunovic fairly replied. 'I wish we could provide them with translations but you must understand that this entire event is financed by the Democratic Party and our financial resources are limited. Those interpreters happen to be Democratic Party members who speak Slovene and Macedonian. Unfortunately we do not have any members who speak Albanian or Hungarian. If we did, we would provide them.' Brushing aside this reasonable explanation Jurica continued with his precise, icy logic. 'While we are on the subject of language, I would also like to request a simultaneous translation of the proceedings into Croatian.' Jurica's request, which would be akin to somebody from Glasgow requesting that a Londoner's speech be translated into Scottish English, provoked uproar and laughter. An avalanche of fists thumped the table, one delegate walked out in disgust never to return, the assembled observers had tears of laughter in their eyes but there was more to come as one of the delegates from Sarajevo stood up and screamed above the commotion in all seriousness, 'I demand a translation into Bosnian!' (the equivalent of Irish English).[136]

It is worth considering whether there is anything the interpreters could have done in this situation to prevent the breakdown in communication.

4 Interpreting under Pressure

Interpreters are expected to remain neutral and must discipline themselves to maintain a minimum of composure and decorum even under stress. An interpreter must identify with the speaker he is interpreting at least enough to render that party's tone and intent, but the interpreter's position becomes untenable if he or she openly displays emotion or sympathy toward one of the parties. For example, a news broadcast of 27 December 1995 reported that, at a trial in Japan of three American soldiers accused of having raped a minor, the testimony was so emotionally charged that the court interpreter 'broke down and cried'. Obviously, whatever the merits of the case, such a display on the part of the interpreter could color or taint some of the evidence. Consider also the following situation, which occurred during a talk between US Ambassador April Glaspie and Iraqi President Saddam Hussein before the outbreak of the Gulf War:

> [US Ambassador:] ...and then we learn that many units of the Republican Guard have been sent to the border? Is it not reasonable for us to ask, in the spirit of friendship, not confrontation, the simple question: What are your intentions?

> Saddam said that was indeed a reasonable question. He acknowledged that we should be concerned for regional peace, in fact it is our duty as a superpower. 'But how can we make them [Kuwait and U.A.E.] understand how deeply we are suffering.' The financial situation is such that the pensions for widows and orphans will have to be cut. **At this point the interpreter and one of the note takers broke down and wept.**[137]

The interpreter's neutrality may also be compromised when he or she is asked to also act as spokesperson or guide, which occasionally happens, especially to escort interpreters. There is nothing unethical about a guide or spokesperson who works for an institution also providing incidental service as an interpreter to the extent they are able. However, a professional interpreter should not accept an assignment that requires the interpreter to propound an 'official line', to indoctrinate listeners, or to censor or distort conversations. This would bring the interpreting profession into disrepute.

5 Interpreters in the Old West (1): W.E.P. Hartnell

The state of California was established in September of 1849 by a constitutional convention which met in Monterey. Of the 48 members in attendance, seven were native Californians (some Spanish-speaking), and five were foreign-born, including one from Spain. 'The convention was organized on September 4th. Robert J. Semple, delegate from Sonoma, was elected president and William G. Marcy was elected secretary. **W.E.P. Hartnell was elected translator for the Spanish-speaking members** and various other lesser officers were elected. J. Ross Browne was elected reporter.'[138]

It appears that Mr. Hartnell was not himself a delegate to the convention. If he had been, should he have been eligible to become translator or would that have constituted a conflict of interest? Should the office of translator or interpreter for a legislative assembly or other official body be an elective office? If so, who should be eligible for the position and who should be entitled to vote for the candidates? What should be the candidates' qualifications and who should define and enforce them? Does the choice of Ross Browne as reporter indicate recognition of the fact that communicating among the parties present at a meeting and communicating the result of the meeting to the world at large are two different things?

Interpreters in the Old West (2): Billy the Kid

BILLY THE KID - By Ben Wittick (1845–1903) – This image is used in several forms on a number of websites. Public Domain, https://commons.wikimedia.org/w/index.php?curid = 1070095

'Billy the Kid's real name was Henry McCarty and he was born to an Irish immigrant family in New York City on 17 September 1859. His early years are still elusive to historians, much is known, but elements of his early life are still unknown. By 1872 his family had moved to Santa Fe, New Mexico, and this is where the legend of Billy the Kid begins. ...

In the late 1870s Mary Coghlan, Pat's niece, came to live at the Three Rivers Ranch. She came straight from Ireland and did not know English at all, her only language was Gaelic. Pat Coghlan did not have enough Gaelic to speak with Mary and her having no English made for a difficult time. **Pat asked Billy the Kid to act as interpreter as Billy knew both languages fluently. On interest, Billy could also speak fluent Spanish, so he was a handy man to have around.** Writer Chuck Usmar discovered Billy's Gaelic language ability while reading through interviews with people who knew the Coghlans and Billy. It is another interesting piece of Old West lore.'[139]

Besides being a skillful gunfighter, it seems that Henry McCarty sometimes earned a living using his language skills. He gained his fluency in Gaelic from his family upbringing and in Spanish through travels in Mexico while engaged in lawful employment. Yet he is famous only as an outlaw.

6 Interpreters on Horseback

During the Spanish conquest of North America, the many expeditions sent out from Mexico City generally included a large contingent of native people who served in various capacities, including that of interpreter, the latter function often combined with that of emissary or courier. 'A typical expedition consisted of a few hundred Spaniards, followed by hordes of natives carrying the baggage, opening roads, performing camp duty, and serving as **couriers and interpreters.**'[140] In October of 1775, a group of settlers travelled from Mexico to California to found the city of San Francisco.

> They numbered 240 persons when they left; including births en route, a death by childbirth, and a few dropouts who settled farther south, 244 settlers arrived. The roster listed 3 officers and a surveyor, 3 Fathers, 18 veteran soldiers and 20 recruits, 29 soldiers' wives plus the rest of their families, 40 families of colonists, ...20 muleteers, 3 men to herd the beef cattle, 4 servants for the Fathers, **and 3 Indian interpreters.**[141]

Why are the interpreters mentioned last on the list, after the muleteers, herdsmen and servants? Is it simply because activities are always considered more important in themselves than communicating about the activities? Were three interpreters enough to service the communication needs of a community of 244 people? Does the number of interpreters employed for this mission, compared to the number of soldiers, suggest that the settlers envisaged having extensive communication with the native Californians? Is it likely that three interpreters were sufficient to cover the sizeable number of languages spoken by the native Californians? Native American interpreters serving as escort interpreters often had to work on horseback in order to accompany their clients to their destinations. What practical difficulties might this present?

Group of Indian guides and interpreters on horseback
From the New York Public Library. Miriam and Ira D. Wallach Division of Art, Prints and Photographs. Photography Collection, The New York Public Library. New York Public Library Digital Collections – http://digitalcollections.nypl.org/items/510d47e0-bb8e-a3d9-e040-e00a18064a99. RIGHTS STATEMENT: The New York Public Library believes that this item is in the public domain under the laws of the United States, but did not make a determination as to its copyright status under the copyright laws of other countries. This item may not be in the public domain under the laws of other countries.

7 Urgency and Speed

In the fall of 1961, Soviet Premier Nikita Khrushchev had a complex proposal concerning the status of Berlin which he wished to communicate to President John F. Kennedy. Khrushchev sent two people to convey the proposal to Kennedy: one to make the proposal, and one to interpret. Georgi Bolshakov, the interpreter, accompanied Soviet envoy Mikhail Kharlamov on a visit to Kennedy's press secretary, Pierre Salinger. Salinger recalls in a memoir that, when Kharlamov began outlining the proposal,

> His words were tumbling out almost faster than Bolshakov could translate. I told him to sit down and take his time.[142]

Salinger made notes on the proposal, which he later communicated to President Kennedy. Kennedy's reaction suggests that the proposal was fully and clearly understood. Would it have been equally well conveyed if one and the same person had been asked to be both envoy and interpreter for Mr. Khrushchev? Does Mr. Kharlamov's speed of delivery suggest anything about the complexity of the proposal? (Do you tend to speak faster when you have several important points to make and are afraid of forgetting one of them?) When a complex proposal has to be both expounded __and__ translated, is there a greater possibility of error or omission? Does the potential for error increase with the urgency of the situation?

8 The Disappearing Interpreter

Generally, it is important to render the speaker's meaning even if some of the rhetorical flavor of the speech is lost in the process. Indeed, in simultaneous interpretation it is sometimes impossible to render the full flavor of the speech, especially if the speaker grows excited and begins speaking too fast. However, an interpreter's style of delivery can distort the speaker's intent. For example, in 1973, then US Secretary of State Henry Kissinger held a luncheon for a group of African and Arab delegates in order to convey to them the general thrust of current US policy. When he finished speaking, Kissinger's remarks were interpreted.

> **The translator, seeking self-effacement, rendered Kissinger's prose in a slight sing-song** that gave the thing the **flavor of a ritual**, like prayers said at the foot of the altar; and of course that is what it was.[143]

While a simultaneous interpreter must sometimes resort to a neutral or flat delivery simply in order to keep up with the speaker's speed, is there any reason why an interpreter working in the __consecutive__ mode should resort to rendering a speech in a 'sing-song'? In the case of a highly articulate speaker, like Henry Kissinger, is not a 'sing-song' delivery especially inappropriate? In this particular case, since Mr. Kissinger apparently read out a prepared statement, could the interpreter's performance have been improved if he or she had requested an advance copy of the speech to work on beforehand, so that he or she could have given more attention to the style and delivery when the time came to interpret the statement? Although 'self-effacement' is a natural and necessary defense-mechanism for interpreters, it does not mean diluting the tone of a statement, or failing to reproduce eloquence when the speaker is eloquent. Consider the following, which occurred during the toasts given at a formal diplomatic dinner hosted by Secretary of State Kissinger in 1973:

> ...Kissinger came through with a quite extraordinarily deft and eloquent few paragraphs. Then there was [General Assembly] President Benites [of Ecuador]... We had to go through it all from Benites. Relaxation of tensions, peace, technology, brotherhood, human aspirations. **The length of it was of course doubled by the translation.** It is an interesting role, the translator's. On the one hand he must be **totally self-effacing**, as anonymous as possible. On the other hand, he cannot transmit the speaker's rhetoric without __some__ deference to the speaker's theatrical devices, tonal and linguistic. But it would hardly do for a lanky twenty-five-year-old Sunday-suited translator to sound like Martin Luther King, in translating

Martin Luther King; to do so would raise eyebrows. Fortunately, Benites is not a florid elocutionist. His prose is very ornate and very meticulous, and the translator chose to relay it matter-of-factly, which was safe, but also, gnashingly soporific, so that we had to pinch ourselves to stay awake. It was finally over, and we ambled out...[144]

Why must the interpreter be 'totally self-effacing'? Is it mainly in order not to upstage the speaker, who is the star of the occasion? Is it in order to preserve professional neutrality? Is it because the interpreter must concentrate completely on the <u>content</u> and sacrifice the style? Or is it due to the limitations of the interpretation process itself? If the speaker has eloquently delivered an important message, and if it is within the interpreter's skill to make the interpretation as eloquent and interesting as the original, is there any reason why he or she should refrain from doing so? At a 1975 meeting of oil-producing countries, although there was nothing dull about the speeches, the interpretation is described as having sounded monotonous:

> [Delegates] sat inside the hall, listening through earphones to the **monotone translation of the stern speeches**: arraigning the 'maneuvers and manipulations of certain powers', emphasizing that 'countries living beyond their means must accept the transformation that is inevitable'...[145]

Does stern rhetoric call for a 'monotone' delivery in interpretation?

At the Beijing Fourth World Conference on Women, Secretary of State Madeleine Albright recalls that the need to process speeches through interpretation into several languages presented a danger of diluting the more lively or inspiring interventions and making them dull, but Hillary Clinton's speech overcame that danger: 'Having done my share of public speaking, I know how hard it is to excite a crowd. It is especially difficult at a conference showcasing a long procession of accomplished orators. I didn't think it possible to arouse the audience in Beijing, which was made up of people from every culture listening to translators mangle the First Lady's grammar in a monotone. But Hillary's speech was a stunner. It was beautifully written and forcefully delivered....'[146]

In the consecutive mode, it is even more important to make the interpretation as interesting as the original, since doubling the time creates the risk of boring the audience even if the speech was a good one.

Do you agree with Mr. Buckley's view that 'it would hardly do' for an interpreter to sound like the speaker? Although the interpreter should not produce a parody or impersonation, why not reproduce the speaker's tone and manner as faithfully as one's acting skill permits?

9 When There is no Interpretation....

The clients and employers of translators and interpreters, be they private or governmental, do not always publicly acknowledge the usefulness or value of translation and interpretation, which they tend to take for granted, and sometimes even treat as a superfluous luxury. Former Prime Minister John Major of the United Kingdom, for example, told the 50th United Nations General Assembly that too much money was being wasted on speeches 'brilliantly interpreted into six languages'. (He was perhaps intimating that it would have been better for the UN's 190+ member states to use English). The professional requirement that translators and interpreters maintain a low profile unfortunately contributes to this state of affairs. A profession whose function requires that its practitioners be 'invisible' cannot engage in very much self-promotion or lobbying.

However, under some circumstances, the presence or absence of a qualified linguist may determine whether a given event or transaction will take place, or who will benefit from it. For example, it appears that in 1901 it was the absence of the Persian interpreter attached to the Russian embassy in Tehran that made it possible for William Knox D'Arcy to gain control over Persian oil supplies for British Petroleum despite potential opposition and competition from Russia:

> [D'Arcy's envoys] 'negotiated with the Grand Vizier in Teheran against some pressure from the Russians and eventually – **taking advantage of the absence of the only Russian in their embassy who could read Persian** – they signed a concession covering 480,000 square miles (nearly twice the size of Texas)...'[147]

Similarly, there is some anecdotal evidence that the impact of the disastrous surprise attack at Pearl Harbor that precipitated the US entry into World War II may have been magnified by communications delay due to the absence of anyone at the Japanese embassy in Washington who could transcribe diplomatic messages from Tokyo with sufficient speed (although this may have been a deliberately contrived 'language barrier').

These incidents pose an interesting ethical problem. If a linguist knows that a course of events is likely to be influenced by the presence or absence of translation or interpretation, should he or she take the initiative to bring that fact to the attention of the parties and enable their communication? If so, which one? If the parties have displayed disregard for linguistic expertise, e.g. by failing to arrange for interpretation or translation, should a translator or interpreter make an effort to spare the parties the consequences of their mistake? (By analogy, does a physician have an ethical duty to diagnose or treat a person who is sick but who does not believe in medicine? Or should a lawyer intercede in favor of a criminal defendant who spurns legal processes and will otherwise remain unrepresented?)

10 Interpreters in Danger Zones

Interpreters are sometimes exposed to risk because they must work in war zones or in settings where adversaries come into contact or where controversial issues are thrashed out. The Armed Forces Journal reported in 2011 that interpreters in Iraq were 'ten times more likely to die in combat than deployed American or international forces.'[148]

However, this element of risk is rarely given recognition. At times it seems almost as if linguists were considered expendable. Consider the following:

On 30 August 1995, NATO aircraft conducted a series of air strikes on Bosnian Serb targets in Bosnia. During this action, two groups of people were captured by the Bosnian Serbs: the crew of a French aircraft, and a team of Spanish peace monitors.

It was reported on the front page of the New York Times the following day that during the attack two French pilots had ejected from their jet. The risk faced by the two pilots was therefore considered highly newsworthy, although it was believed they had survived. Another story which was considered sufficiently newsworthy to appear the same day on page 16 was the fact that three European Union peace monitors had been reported killed near Sarajevo. The story said that 'Three Spanish peace monitors and two other people were killed near Sarajevo...' Only from an incidental observation in a related story on page 16 does one learn who these 'other people' were: 'Achieving peace in the notoriously treacherous Balkans will be especially difficult if allied losses become numerous. Five Spaniards – two military observers, a diplomat, a driver and an interpreter – were killed today and a French Mirage jet was shot down, with its two-man crew reportedly parachuting before it crashed'. The EU interpreter was reported to have been killed, but that was considered less important than the fact that two pilots bailed out of their plane. It was also considered less important than the deaths of the diplomat and the two military observers. In fact, the interpreter is only listed in the story after the driver of the vehicle, seemingly as an afterthought. (It was later reported that the EU team had not been killed but 'only abducted' by Bosnian Serb forces.)

Similarly, it was only as an incidental human-interest note long after the event that CNN News reported the death of Ms. Julie Marie Welch, a Spanish interpreter working in the Social Security office in the Oklahoma City federal building when that building was blown up by a terrorist on 19 April 1995. The focus of the story was her father's grief and the sympathy shown to him by many people who had written him letters of condolences, but there was no hint of recognition of Ms. Welch's acceptance of the public service ethic or the risks accompanying her profession.

Turning to a different part of the world, the brutal murder of Hitoshi Igarashi, the Japanese translator of Salman Rushdie's *The Satanic Verses*, pursuant to a fatwa by Ayatollah Khomeini, also received only incidental treatment in the press, the main thrust of the stories being the danger faced by the author himself, although he was under constant police protection.

Hitoshi Igarashi
Photo from Wikipedia.

What conclusion can one draw from these incidents about the value of an interpreter's life in the opinion of the general public and the press? What is the reason for the interpreter's lack of social standing? What might interpreters do to enhance the prestige of their profession or to gain due recognition of the risks they take? What personal precautions should an interpreter take if faced with a hazardous assignment?

11 Danger: Amateurs at Work

There is an unfortunate tendency to leave decisions about translation and interpretation to the last minute and then to make do with anyone at hand who claims to 'speak the language'. This occurs even in situations calling for the utmost clarity and accuracy. The use of a novice interpreter can also lead to serious misunderstandings and incongruities of speech register or idiom, which not only do a disservice to the principals but also place the interpreting profession in an unfavorable light.

In the following incident, which occurred during the US occupation of Germany, an amateur interpreter turned a speech that was intended to sound stern and admonitory into one which sounded absurdly funny to its intended audience.

> There were about fifty Russian officers present, including a few generals and a number of Soviet WACS. In characteristic fashion [Major General Ernest] Harmon was verbally attacking his Russian guests for their tendency to treat Americans like potential enemies instead of allies. Harmon had located an American lieutenant from Brooklyn whose parents had emigrated from Russia, and he was **using this young man as his interpreter**. The lad obviously was anxious to please his commander, but 'Hell on Wheels' Harmon suspected the interpreter was toning down his purple remarks. Several times Harmon broke off to say to the lieutenant in a loud voice, 'If you don't translate my exact words, so help me, I'll bust you!'

Thus exhorted to use Russian equivalents for the General's salty phrases, the interpreter produced all the emphatic words he had ever heard in Brooklyn, including some profanity – and the effect upon the listening Russians, especially the WACS, was sensational. Continuous roars and shouts of laughter filled the hall, to the perplexity of Harmon who was very much in earnest.[149]

Major General Ernest N. Harmon

What does this incident suggest about the relationship between an interpreter and his / her principal? Was this young recruit the right person to act as interpreter for an officer who was known to his troops as 'old gravel voice'?

Rarely is it as important to properly render a speaker's tone as in military contexts. This situation, like others requiring specific skills, should be addressed through specific training. For example, during a training course conducted by the author for military escort interpreters, trainees were taught how to adopt a duly respectful tone when addressing village elders, how a commander's order to troops is expected to sound, and how emergency directions given by a military officer to civilians in danger are supposed to sound, with illustrative examples performed in the classroom by a military officer.

Since persons using an interpreter are doing so because they do not speak the target language, should they take it upon themselves to intervene in order to correct the interpreter's accuracy? In most cases, probably not. On the other hand, when it is obvious that an interpreter is not conveying the intended tone, what else can a speaker do but complain to the interpreter? But should such complaints be made during the interpreter's performance, since they are sure to aggravate an amateur interpreter's nervousness?

An interpreter must, however, be alert to the real motive behind a speaker's critique of his performance, since such motives may not always be pure. In some situations it is required that a foreign party be interpreted into the language of the proceeding even if the party understands that language, which puts that person in a position to monitor and criticize the interpretation. He may then assume the right to intervene and tell the interpreter how to do his job, to gain advantage by discrediting the interpreter's performance. The interpreter should invoke the forum's authority if this happens and respond with firmness to stop attempted disruptions.

Interpreter Richard Sonnenfeldt, who served at the Nuremberg trials, had to deal with such an uncooperative witness, as his son recalls in this anecdote:

> My father's most important interrogation was when he interviewed Goering, the highest ranking Nazi official that had been captured. Goering understood English but was a bully who would constantly berate and mock the translators. My father was 23 years old when he met Goering for the first time. During that meeting my father translated something that Goering had said to Col. Amen. When Goering attempted to correct my father, he replied, 'Herr Gerink' – a pun he had heard as a child, meaning, 'little nothing' – 'when I translate the colonel's question into German and your answers into English, you keep quiet until I am finished...' Goering gave my father a long look and replied, 'My name is Goering, not Gerink!' [But my father's] stern rebuke was appreciated by Goering who, from then on, demanded that only my father be his translator.[150]

12 Hitler's Interpreter

Interpreters operate under considerable psychological stress due to the technical demands of the job. In addition, they may also be subjected to psychological, moral and/or economic pressures by their employers. The following is an example of an interpreter who seems to have found himself trapped 'for the duration' in a morally objectionable and psychologically nerve-racking job:

> On 31 March 1971 the B.B.C. broadcast an interview by Donald McLachlan, a former editor of the Sunday Telegraph, with the linguist Paul Schmidt. Schmidt had a working knowledge of as many as twenty languages, but what deserves more interest is that from 1933 to 1945 he was Adolf Hitler's personal interpreter. In that function he was **present at almost all of Hitler's conferences**, ably translating and minuting all that was said. More than that, **it was he who received the British ultimatum to Hitler in 1939, presented the German ultimatum to the Russians two years later and prepared the deportation of Hungarian Jews in 1943.** He became, as he remarked with a smile, 'a piece of Hitler's furniture'.

Hitler's interpreter, Dr. Paul Schmidt (center, in leather coat), translates for Hitler and Romanian dictator Ion Antonescu (at far left). Photo from National Archives and Records Administration (ushmm.org)

http://www.librarything.com/pic/165045

Although **he had a dislike for Hitler from the beginning,** Schmidt accepted the job of interpreter because of what he described as the interesting perspectives offered by high-level diplomacy. He would be able to travel widely and to meet the world's political leaders on the most momentous occasions. In the interview he recalled with remarkable relish how at lunches or dinners he managed both to translate and to eat by always taking small bites at a time. Even when, with keen psychological insight, he recognized the baseness of his employer's tactics, **he could not bring himself to give expression to his disgust and resign from his post.** In that case, he explained, **Hitler would simply have said: 'But next week Chamberlain is coming!' or something like that.**[151]

Do you agree with the author of the above comment that Mr. Schmidt could simply have 'resigned' from the Third Reich after having been privy to 'almost all of Hitler's conferences'? Would he have been allowed simply to walk away?

Like many Germans, Mr. Schmidt was probably not fully aware of Hitler's ultimate plans as early as 1933, when he began working for Hitler. However, by 1937, when Hitler had made his intentions abundantly clear, and certainly by 1943 when Mr. Schmidt's work included 'preparing the deportation of Hungarian Jews', he must have been aware of the moral implications of what he was doing by continuing to collaborate with this employer. Should he then have attempted to resign or escape (assuming that was possible)? Or did he have a duty, as an interpreter, to stay at his post for the duration? Is an interpreter who has been present during hostilities the one best qualified to interpret in the eventual peace negotiations? Or does familiarity with the events, on the contrary, make that person less objective?

Could it have been not just his 'insider' knowledge, but also his 'working knowledge of as many as twenty languages' that made Mr. Schmidt seemingly so valuable to his employer? Does a 'working knowledge' of a language qualify an interpreter to use that language in high-level work?

What steps might one take as a translator or interpreter to avoid being trapped in a job that proves to be morally compromising? How can an interpreter best preserve his or her personal and economic independence?

Was it a breach of professional ethics for Mr. Schmidt to accept a BBC interview in 1971 and talk about his past experiences, 30 years after the events? As the person who not only interpreted but also wrote the minutes for Hitler's conferences, was he especially qualified to perform the function of a historical chronicler?

In the United Nations, translators are also trained to be précis-writers. Should interpreting and minute-writing be performed by the same person? With the availability of modern recording equipment, is it necessary any longer for hand-written minutes of meetings to be taken?

Do you agree with the author of the above comment that Mr. Schmidt's conduct was 'servile'? When many Germans far more powerful than Mr. Schmidt were unable to 'express their disgust and resign' without fear of reprisals, what would have happened to 'a mere translator'?

Do you agree with M. Jean Herbert, author of *The Interpreter's Handbook*, that an interpreter is obligated to perform the work he has contractually agreed to do and therefore should not take responsibility for the content of the speeches he translates?

Would you consider that Mr. Schmidt redeemed himself for his collaboration with Hitler by testifying against Ribbentrop at the Nuremberg trials? When Mr. Schmidt testified to the effect that the Nazis were bent on conquest from the start, was that testimony consistent with his own innocence? Was it merely a statement of the obvious, made after the war, with the benefit of hindsight?

Mr. Schmidt presumably testified not as an expert witness but as an ordinary citizen who had witnessed certain events. However, he witnessed those events in his professional capacity. Should testimony about statements made in the presence of an interpreter sworn to professional secrecy be admissible in court? Should such statements be considered hearsay?

Should an interpreter ever be required by law to reveal the secrets of his or her clients? Or should interpreters enjoy the same professional privilege enjoyed by lawyers or doctors?

Do you agree with the decision of the Nuremberg War Crimes Tribunal, which acquitted Mr. Schmidt?

At important meetings lasting over an hour with simultaneous interpretation, the standard interpreting team is at least two people. Should a single interpreter working alone ever agree to perform diplomatic functions in combination with interpreting assignments? Are diplomatic or interpreting functions jeopardized by asking one person to combine the two? Should it be part of the interpreter's work to serve as a messenger in order to receive or deliver ultimatums? Conversely, are diplomatic or negotiating functions compatible with performing multilingual communication competently?

To perform her function properly, a diplomatic interpreter strives to enable the parties to communicate 'as if she wasn't there' (See e.g.: http://www.spiegel.de/karriere/von-beruf-dolmetscherin-uebersetzen-ist-ihr-job-a-1037378.html). Burdening such an interpreter with additional functions, such as that of record-keeper or historical chronicler, observer or eyewitness, would undermine her ability to perform the main function, which depends on total focus and concentration upon what is being said by the interlocutors. Is an interpreter who is transformed after the fact into an unwilling witness actually being turned into a spy? What would be the practical, legal and diplomatic implications of using interpreters for espionage in that manner?

Consider the situation faced by the American interpreter who was assigned to interpret for President Donald Trump at his confidential bilateral meeting in Helsinki of 19 July 2018 with Vladimir Putin and who later faced calls by US legislators to respond to questions about what was said at that meeting. Here are some headlines about that event and the continuing debate that has ensued:

Trump's interpreter: Should she be compelled to tell what she heard during private meeting with Putin?
https://www.usatoday.com/story/news/politics/2018/07/19/helsinki-summit-democrats-want-hear-trumps-interpreter/799733002/

Trump's Helsinki performance puts translator in the spotlight
https://www.cnn.com/2018/07/18/politics/trump-russian-translator-spotlight/index.html

Trump-Putin Firestorm Brings Interpreters Out From the Shadows
https://foreignpolicy.com/2018/07/19/trump-putin-firestorm-brings-interpreters-out-from-the-shadows-europe-diplomacy-state-department-russia-president-election-interference-congress-subpoena/

See also: Helena Kaschel, *Interpreters make really lousy spies – interview with Isabella Gusenburger.* DW.com, 3 January 2019.

https://www.dw.com/en/interpreters-make-really-lousy-spies/a-46954
023?fbclid=IwAR1kE461V0JhYkuoVm67edFHPd1vWCfsNnPcmM6Q7
ZqLC4wTrLILJ9ljhd8

Note that the position of the International Association of Conference Interpreters on this matter calls for complete and absolute confidentiality. The reasons are well explained in this article by Christopher Thiery: *Total et absolu : le secret professionnel*

https://aiic.net/page/8672/total-et-absolu-le-secret-professionnel/lang/2?
fbclid=IwAR1Lpm7mY4_GLdt-pMv7fdzXbYMv2mUM1JKvCv_i1rIIDvihu
JvYWJr9ehI

See also: Tara Palmer & Benjamin Siegel, *Interpreter from Trump-Putin summit may be forced into congressional spotlight,* NBC News, 14 January 2019. US newsmedia continue to erroneously assume that interpreters memorize past conversations overheard and that their notes preserve the content of confidential statements like the transcript of a court reporter. Thus, the media debate whether the interpreter could be lawfully compelled to 'testify' about her 'knowledge' of what was the parties said despite the obvious objection that it would be hearsay, insinuate that the interpreter's contractual status circumscribes her professional ethics, and read evasive intent into the fact that the interpreter handed over her notes to the parties at the end of the meeting, which is done routinely upon request. It would be ironic, unfair, dangerous and counterproductive if vital multilingual diplomatic discussions were hampered because interpreters could not be trusted to maintain the same confidentiality that is taken for granted when two interlocutors speak the same language.

https://abcnews.go.com/Politics/interpreter-trump-putin-summit-
forced-congressional-spotlight/story?id=60352635&cid=share_facebook_
widget&fbclid=IwAR0fwmcsncGwoBDExqerJj6HS7BvvuRE-483Qf6FRI
2Js50QDMSuPLvtvz4

In India, the need for Hindi specialists to interpret when Prime Minister Narendra Modi used the language in conversations with foreign counterparts has sometimes led to assigning the task to diplomats, resulting in controversy in the Indian Parliament.

Diplomats Donning Interpreter Caps Draws Parliamentary Panel Concern

By Devirupa Mitra

New Indian Express - Published: 27th December 2015 04:32 AM / Updated: 27th December 2015 04:32 AM

http://www.newindianexpress.com/nation/Diplomats-Donning-Inter
preter-Caps-Draws-Parliamentary-Panel-Concern/2015/12/27/article
3197756.ece

NEW DELHI: A parliamentary panel has frowned upon Indian diplomats doubling up as interpreters, a practice which gained momentum due to the need for Hindi specialists when Prime Minister
Narendra Modi used the language in conversations with foreign
counterparts.

The leg up for hiring additional Hindi interpreters has come from
the Shashi Tharoor-led Parliamentary Standing Committee on
External Affairs. The observation came on the heels of the Ministry
of External Affairs (MEA) arguing that Indian Foreign Service (IFS)
officers were being used as interpreters during VVIP visits.

'The Committee... are of the strong view that the present arrangement where IFS officers play the role of interpreters is compromising
the quality of the actual performance of IFS officers as well as the job
of interpretation,' said the committee report, submitted during
Parliament's winter session. [...]

13 Recognition of Interpreting as a Profession: A Long March

Recognition of diplomatic interpreting as a modern profession has
made notable strides but was at first slow to come. The following
moving profile of a master interpreter vividly brings out the challenges
that have often confronted interpreters working in the international
political arena especially during the Cold War, the difficulty of maintaining professional impartiality, and the personal sacrifices that this
effort may imply.

In China, professional interpreters have long played an important
part in conducting the country's diplomatic relations. Mr. Ji Chaozhu,
for example, served for more than 20 years as English interpreter for
Chinese leaders, particularly Chairman Mao Zedong. When US President
Richard Nixon visited Beijing in 1972, it was the first time an American
president had been in China since the founding of the People's Republic
in 1949 and an important diplomatic stepping-stone towards normalizing
relations with China. Mr. Nixon was met at the airport by Prime Minister
Zhou Enlai, who instructed his interpreter, Mr. Ji, to stand directly
behind him and listen attentively, as the meeting was taking place in the
relatively noisy setting of an airport tarmac. Archival memoranda from
the period, like the one below, show that specific interpreters were
selected by name to serve at these high-level meetings, in this case Tang
Wen-sheng. They also show that the Chinese interpreter was deft in han-
dling humorous niceties, one of the more difficult and important aspects

of diplomatic discourse, as it is often used to 'break the ice'. The memorandum also reveals that producing notes of the meeting was not a task assigned to the interpreter; instead it was done by one of the diplomats, Mr. Winston Lord.

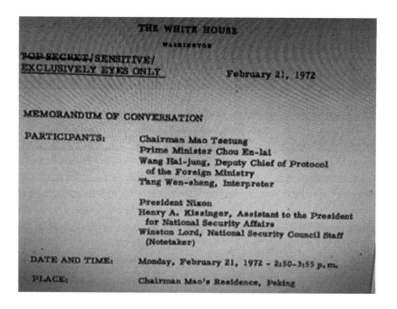

THE WHITE HOUSE
WASHINGTON

TOP SECRET/SENSITIVE/
EXCLUSIVELY EYES ONLY   February 21, 1972

MEMORANDUM OF CONVERSATION

PARTICIPANTS: Chairman Mao Tsetung
                     Prime Minister Chou En-lai
                     Wang Hai-jung, Deputy Chief of Protocol
                        of the Foreign Ministry
                     Tang Wen-sheng, Interpreter

                     President Nixon
                     Henry A. Kissinger, Assistant to the President
                        for National Security Affairs
                     Winston Lord, National Security Council Staff
                        (Notetaker)

DATE AND TIME: Monday, February 21, 1972 - 2:50-3:55 p.m.

PLACE: Chairman Mao's Residence, Peking

Public domain image from website of the Nixon Foundation.
https://www.nixonfoundation.org/exhibit/the-opening-of-china/

See also:

The Man on Mao's Right, at the Center of History

By David Barboza

New York Times, 17 February 2012

http://www.nytimes.com/2012/02/18/world/asia/ji-chaozhu-man-on-maos-right-at-center-of-history.html

---

In China, the stature and public image of diplomatic interpreters have evolved considerably thanks to effective high-level training and to the wider exposure created by media and internet coverage. Conference interpreting has even become the leitmotif of a popular television program, '*The Interpreter*', which recently drew 100 million viewers in one week. The Hunan TV-produced drama has become extremely popular since it first aired in 2016. The program's Chinese title 亲爱的翻译官 (Qin Ai De Fan Yi Guan) translates roughly into 'Dear Translation Official.' (The Chinese 翻译 (Fan Yi) can refer to both translation and interpretation.)[152]

14 A Notorious Interpreting Misunderstanding

The Russian phrase 'Мы вас похороним', meaning 'We shall inter you' (i.e. we shall be present at your funeral) was used by former Soviet premier Nikita Khrushchev to an audience of Western diplomats at a reception at the Polish embassy in Moscow on 18 November 1956. The speaker's intent was to assert that the Soviet system was superior and would outlive the Western system, as is shown by the previous sentence, which was 'Whether you like it or not, history is on our side'. The remark, while boastful, was not meant to be disrespectful, as is shown by the fact that nowadays Russian bloggers use the same expression to discuss how Lenin should be laid to rest, while using a different verb to propose that he should be buried.[153] The author himself heard the claim 'our system is better than yours' more than once from Russian colleagues at the UN. However, Mr. Khrushchev's rhetorical jibe was widely misinterpreted and misconstrued in the context of cold-war tensions as a kind of macabre death threat and was rendered loosely into English in Western news stories as 'We will bury you'. Moreover, in anecdotal reporting and discussion about incident, the remark is sometimes blamed on the interpreter who was working for Mr. Khrushchev at the event, Viktor Sukhodrev, and it has even been suggested that a subsequent souring of East–West relations over the next ten years was the fault of this 'translation mistake'. Yet, the same interpreter was still working at US-Soviet summits 17 years later, even in bilateral talks where he was the only third party present, a practice which is viewed as a mark of strong confidence in an interpreter's ability.[154]

Viktor Sukhodrev – 'In a career of nearly thirty years, Sukhodrev was present at numerous high-profile summits and deal-makings. Richard Nixon called Sukhodrev 'a superb linguist who spoke English as well as he did Russian',[1] while Henry Kissinger called him 'unflappable' and a 'splendid interpreter'.[2] According to *International Herald Tribune*, 'Sukhodrev was present but not present, emptying himself of ego, slipping into the skin of the man who was speaking, feeling his feelings, saying his words'.[3]'

[https://en.wikipedia.org/wiki/Viktor_Sukhodrev]

Can the purported misinterpretation of Mr. Khrushchev's remark be fairly attributed to a diplomatic interpreter of the caliber of

Mr. Sukhodrev? Or is it more likely a deliberate misrepresentation attributable to a sensationalist press? If it was the latter, should not a correction have been published in the press out of respect for the interpreter's reputation, as happens when an important speaker is inadvertently misquoted? Mr. Sukhodrev's interpretation may have been an attempt to match the tone of Mr. Khrushchev's somewhat brash rhetorical style, but if Mr. Sukhodrev's rendition had been milder in tone, would he not have been accused by the same critics of 'watering down' what they perceived as a threat? Was this incident a case of misinterpretation, political misunderstanding due to cold-war rivalry, or journalistic misrepresentation and sensationalism? Compare this incident with the case of General Harmon described above and with the case of the MONUSCO staff member described below.

15 A Mistranslation Leads to a Tense Standoff

'Here is a real incident that occurred in MONUSCO[155] a few years ago to a UN team, and that could be useful to present here as a "lesson learned" when it comes to working with Language assistant (LA). A Team composed of civil affairs and MILOBS officers was to trying to make an inquiry about an ambush where some people had been robbed and some of them killed. The UN Team was tasked to find out any relevant information about this drama and decided to meet with the toughest rebel group stationed in the area. The UN Team leader was speaking in English, the 1st LA was translating in Arabic, the 2nd LA was retranslating in a local dialect and the 3rd one was translating in the local language spoken by the rebel group. The UN Team started progressively, with greetings and small talk. After one hour of socialization, the Team leader put the question on the table for which they came. "You are the strongest group in the area. For sure, you can help us by telling us who perpetrated the crime". After the three LAs finished their translation, the atmosphere suddenly changed, no more smiles, closed expressions on their faces. To top it all off, the Team leader felt the cold barrel cold of a gun behind his head. After one long minute of frozen situation, the chief of the rebels started to laugh and to talk with the others. As he knew a little bit of Arabic, he pointed out that the 1st LA mistranslated the UN sayings; instead of the original meaning, he translated: "I know you did perpetrate the crime". (UN CIMIC – STM, 2014). Based on the foregoing, it is possible to have two hypotheses: either the language assistant failed during the process of translation/interpretation for not mastering both working languages or the LA refrained from impartiality, which is a must, and then decided to value-judge the situation by blaming the rebels for the crime. It is equally important that users of the service of interpretation, provided by the 130 language assistants in peace missions, always talk to the LAs, establishing criteria and modus operandi to be followed during the events in order to avoid potential collateral damage, which might result in an unexpectedly dangerous situation.'[156]

16 Translation as an Agent of Cultural Growth: A Greek Slave-Poet Translates his Way to Roman Citizenship

During its early days, the culture of Rome consisted almost entirely of works celebrating great national events and books of tradition and ritual. The first important work to depart from those themes was the product of interpretation, translation and adaptation from Greek:

> The first to venture beyond narrowly practical topics was Livius Andronicus, a Greek slave who had been taken prisoner during the sacking of Taranto and taken to Rome, where he recited the Odyssey to his patron's friends. They enjoyed it greatly and, being people of high station, commissioned him to extract from the Odyssey a play for the great *ludes*, or games of the year 240. To translate those Greek verses, Livius reinvented them in Latin, with a rough and irregular rhyme. And in that style he composed a tragedy in which he himself recited and sang all the roles so long as there was a hint of voice left in his throat. The Romans had never before seen the like of this and were so pleased that the government granted recognition to poets as a citizenship category and allowed them to form a 'corporation' with its seat at the Temple of Minerva in Aventino.[157]

What conclusions could one draw from the above episode about the capacity of translation to stimulate cultural growth? Was it the poetic genius of Livius Andronicus that inspired such generous appreciation among the Romans, or was it his skill as a translator? Does the text of a work, independently of its stylistic merit, take on a certain novelty simply by the fact of being translated from another language?

Are linguistic matters mainly private, or are they mainly a matter of public interest and public policy? Is choice of language an issue of freedom expression? Is it a human right? If governments have the power to confer official status on a particular language as the 'official language' of the country, do they also have the power to legislate multilingualism or to confer official recognition on translation and interpretation as a profession? If so, how should this be done? Through official testing and certification, through standard-setting by a national 'academy', or through the formation of an officially recognized corporation or union, as the Romans did for poets?

It seems that for certain languages and at certain times translation may be the only way in which a particular author, no matter how important, may become known to the world beyond his home country and native language, which makes translation an essential channel for the dissemination of knowledge. In the 16th century, 'Standard classical authors were the safest investment for both book publishers and book buyers. In Europe, by the end of the sixteenth century, when there were 263 Latin editions of Virgil, there were also 72 translations into Italian, 27 into French, 11 into English, 5 into German, 5 into Spanish, and 2 into Flemish. Some classical authors became better known in translation than in the original. Plato, for example, was widely read in the Latin translation by Marsilio Ficino (five times reprinted in France before 1550), well before the complete Greek text was published in France in 1678.' [158]

Are there other examples in which translation and/or interpretation have had a major historical impact in encouraging the spread of ideas or bringing about cultural change?

Suggested further reading

Jessner, U. and Kramsch, C. (eds) (2015) *The Multilingual Challenge: Cross-disciplinary Perspectives* Berlin / Boston: De Gruyter, Mouton.
Lim, L., Stroud, C. and Wee, L. (Eds) (2018) *The Multilingual Citizen: Towards a Politics of Language for Agency and Change*. Multilingual Matters, Bristol / Blue Ridge Summit.

17 'I don't speak the language' – The Language Barrier Used as a Shield/Translation and Interpretation as a Key to Ascertaining Truth

Situations arise in which a party may try to ignore, obscure or misrepresent events by claiming that he does not speak a language well enough to correctly understand what happened or what was said. The assertion may serve as a smoke-screen to prevent the truth from coming out, and the party using the pretext may try to portray himself as someone so concerned with fidelity to the facts that he is mistrustful of translation.

At a press conference on 27 November 2018 a US Ambassador was asked why he had not listened to the recording of the death of Saudi-American journalist Jamal Kashoggi, who was killed while in a Saudi embassy in Turkey.[159] 'No, I haven't listened to it,' he said. 'Why do you think I should? What do you think I'll learn from it? Unless you speak Arabic, what are you going to get from it? I don't speak Arabic,' he insisted.

Given the ready availability of interpretation for those needing to review media recordings of events, is it reasonable to disregard an event because one does not speak the language of a participant in the event?

The ambassador implied that he could learn as much about this event from reading a transcript. Given the nature of the event (an extrajudicial killing) could a real transcript exist and would it be a reliable source?

In a situation in which a victim may be screaming or pleading for his life, would a translated transcript be as faithful to the event as an interpretation of a recording done by a trained interpreter?

8 The Status of English in The European Union and as a World Language

> *Viewed freely, the English language is the accretion and growth of every dialect, race and range of time, and is both the free and compacted composition of all.* – Walt Whitman[160]
> *The language of Europe is translation.* –Umberto Eco[161]

Brexit and Standard English: A Discussion Paper – *by James Nolan, JD, AIIC, ACI*[162]

As a member of AIIC and an EU Auxiliary Conference Interpreter, I received an invitation to the General Assembly of EP Permanent and Temporary Staff Interpreters, but I will be unable to attend because I am not in Brussels. However, wishing to offer some input into the discussion of the recent UK vote on separation from the EU, I submit this discussion paper.

The EU is reportedly urging the UK to complete withdrawal procedures expeditiously in order to minimize the disruption caused by Brexit. Meanwhile, there is speculation that English may cease to be used as an official EU language.[163] That would be a misfortune for both the EU and the world.

Britain has no monopoly on the English language, which is part of the world's cultural heritage. I cannot help reflecting that on the occasions when I have been privileged to work for the European Union, training interpreters in the EU Rule of Law Mission in Kosovo organized by the Civilian Office, European Union Special Representative (September, 2009) and interpreting at the 67th EU/US Inter-parliamentary Meeting in Washington D.C. & New York (December, 2009), and translating case documents for the EU Court of Justice (2018), the language I have used was Standard English and knowledge of the dialect of the British Isles was irrelevant.

Regardless of whether England remains a member country, the EU needs English in order to remain what it is today: an intergovernmental organization of global stature representing the values and ideals of European culture, an economic power comparable to the US, and a cornerstone of world order second only to the UN. With the UK gone, the EU will remain all of these things but it would be unrealistic and unfair to ask Ireland or Malta to champion the continued use of English when that position could place them at odds with the survival of their other national languages.[164]

That is how the question appears from a political point of view and it will no doubt be resolved by negotiation. However, the question from a technical-linguistic point of view is somewhat different. English needs to be maintained among the EU languages not out of deference to any particular sovereign state but because for historical reasons it happens to be today's global lingua franca, the nearest thing the world has at this time to a universal language, and hence an invaluable tool of communication, and an indispensable pivot language in simultaneous interpretation into other languages. That being so, it is pointless to expect Anglophone EU linguists to belong to a particular nationality, especially in view of the fact that nationality is per se a suspect classification in most legal contexts because it lends itself to misuse. More importantly, it would also be counterproductive from the standpoint of interpretation quality.

Interpreting is a form of public speaking, and interpreting for international fora, with participants coming from many different nations and cultures and the output being recorded and eventually broadcast online worldwide, is a form of acting on the world stage. Above all else, what is expected of interpreters by an international audience, and by the other interpreters who may be taking relay into other languages, especially if one's target language is a lingua franca like English, is clarity. This means cultivating a relatively neutral style of speech unencumbered by strong accents or regionalisms. In this regard, there is no better advice than that offered by a great actress and acting teacher, Uta Hagen:

> Hamlet's advice to the players, 'Speak the speech, I pray you, as I pronounced it to you, trippingly on the tongue,' does not make much sense when delivered with New Yorkese distortions. We have heard the comic overtones, the disservice done to the poetry of Christopher Fry and T. S. Eliot, to the tirades of Shaw by drawls and twangs and slurs. Nor is British speech the answer. It places Chekhov, Ibsen, Strindberg or Molière in the heart of England. British speech belongs to our colleagues abroad. If it is demanded by a specific character or the milieu of the play, it can be learned with the relative ease with which other dialects or accents are learned for particular roles.[165]

With or without England, Europe needs English if its voice is to be heard.

9 Interview with James Nolan

Translator/Interpreter of the Month, May 2013

First appeared in: Le-mot-juste-en-anglais.com *(LMJ)*

http://www.le-mot-juste-en-anglais.com/2013/05/traducteurinterprete-du-mois-de-mai-2013-james-nolan.html

French version: https://www.le-mot-juste-en-anglais.com/2013/06/index.html

Photo by author.

LMJ: You come from a cosmopolitan family and you grew up in several countries, before you settled down in the United States. Tell us about that.

James N: My father, a US Navy officer, came from Nova Scotia and my mother, an artist, from Asturias. I was born in the US at the end of World War II and shortly thereafter my family moved to Mexico City where my father did his Masters in Spanish. Both my parents were bilingual and I was raised speaking both languages. Later we lived in Venezuela and Chile before settling in California, where Spanish is also widely spoken. While at the University of California, I also spent summers in Guadalajara, where my parents lived during most of their retirement years.

LMJ: You are a qualified lawyer and you practiced law for a short period in New York. But your career began and continued in the field of interpreting, with a strong focus on legal interpreting. Your language strengths would presumably have stood you in good stead for either of those professions, but what induced you to choose interpreting over law?

James N: In New York City I did linguistic work for several law firms and worked as a lawyer with one of them, but as a lawyer I was one among thousands of lawyers in an overpopulated and extremely competitive field. However, as an interpreter I was among the best, so I decided to remain one. At the UN, I concentrated on international law and human rights issues, volunteering each year to interpret in the General Assembly's Legal Committee. I was promoted to head the language service of an international tribunal and later became Deputy Director of my division, where I also assumed some legal and administrative duties.

LMJ: To take the UN Competitive Examination, you went to study at Geneva University, which was the leading educational institution offering a diploma in international interpreting and translating at the time. In what languages were studies conducted? How did you fare in the UN Examination?

James N: Translation and interpretation courses at the University of Geneva were given in the students' target and source languages, in my case English, French and Spanish. International economics was taught in English and international relations was taught in French. International terminology was taught in four languages (English, French, Spanish and German). Stylistics and précis-writing were taught in English and French. Many of my professors were UN linguists, and there were some very distinguished visiting lecturers, such as Constantin Andronikov, former interpreter of Charles de Gaulle. On graduating, I passed the UN *Concours* and went to the UN in 1977. In 1979 I was selected to join the in-house interpreter training program and received interpreter training from Guido Gómez de Silva and Bruce Boeglin, two of the best diplomatic interpreters.

LMJ: Tell us about your career as a United Nations Interpreter, the languages in which you worked.

James N: Staff interpreters at the UN are in the booth every day, working 7 or 8 meetings per week. To ensure accuracy and fidelity, we work into our strongest language (mother tongue or language of higher education) from two other UN languages (Arabic, Chinese, English, French, Russian, Spanish). I worked into English from Spanish and French. The meetings in which I worked involved a great variety of topics and perspectives, from regional crises and decolonization to the environment and renewable energy sources. The work was sometimes stressful but always interesting. Interpretation is critical to the success of multilateral relations. During the 20 years of my career from 1982 to 2002 my assignments included 6 landmark global events which could not have taken place without simultaneous interpretation, since coverage of the languages of the 190+ countries in the world requires using all 6 UN official languages: the United Nations Conference on the Law of the Sea in 1982 adopted the largest treaty in history governing the world's oceans; the first Summit Meeting of the UN Security Council in 1992 marked the end of the Cold War; the United Nations Conference on Environment and Development ('Earth Summit') in 1992 led the way to the environmental revolution; the Special Commemorative Meeting of 1995 marked the 50th Anniversary of the UN; the Conference of Plenipotentiaries on the Establishment of an International Criminal Court in 1998 codified the Nuremberg precedent on war crimes and crimes against humanity, so that such crimes can now be prosecuted internationally; and the International Conference on Financing for Development in 2002 set the scene for today's economic development system. The issues addressed at those conferences required consensus-based global solutions, since every country in the world had a stake in the outcome.

Each of those conferences arrived at a result that represented a step forward in resolving the issues it had addressed, and that progress could not have been achieved but for the possibility of exhaustively discussing issues in depth, using languages that all participants could understand. It is fascinating, as an interpreter, to have a front-row seat at events such as those, where history is being made and a way to the future is being charted, and to see how multilingual communication contributes to the process.

LMJ: Do you have any particular memories of statesmen for whom you interpreted (and those whom you may have met) and other highlights (as well as possible hitches) in your work as an interpreter at the UN?

James N: There are so many memories... At every General Assembly, a senior UN interpreter will interpret several speeches by heads of state or foreign ministers. I was often asked to interpret the presidents of Bolivia, Peru and Argentina, and sometimes to translate their written speeches. One of the most amiable and courteous statesmen I met was President Ernesto Samper Pizano, for whom I interpreted in 1996 at some bilateral talks. He invited me to lunch during the talks, commended me on my work, and kindly left me with a beautiful memento: a book of aerial photographs of Colombia. This thoughtful gift symbolizes for me the kind of perspective that an interpreter should have of the world around him.

However, from a technical standpoint, the most interesting and challenging assignments I did were press conferences and interviews by President Jacques Chirac in Paris, interpreted live in New York at the Reuters Financial News Studio, in 1995. When you interpret live for a global television audience, the level of concentration required of you is tremendous. But I have to say that the satellite feed and technical arrangements set up by Reuters were impeccable: it was as if the speaker and I were in the same room. Moreover, M. Chirac is an excellent speaker and it is truly a pleasure to interpret someone who handles the French language so deftly.

LMJ: Under the UN mandatory retirement policy your UN appointment expired when you turned 60. Since then your career has taken off in other directions and you receive invitations from different parts of the world to teach and conduct seminars and courses, principally for conference interpreters. You also serve as a consultant. Where have you been invited? Are the courses one-time events? What is the level of the students whom you teach in these courses? Are those courses confined to English-Spanish-French speakers? For which bodies do you consult?

James N: I have been invited to teach or lecture in Canada, Germany, Kosovo, Argentina and South Africa. In the US, I have taught or lectured in New York, Washington D.C., California, Florida, Colorado, Wisconsin, North Carolina, Idaho and Hawaii. My seminars in Canada and South Africa have become regular events, and I have made three trips to Kosovo as a consultant to prepare training courses and to train linguists for the OSCE Mission in Kosovo and the European Union legal mission, EULEX.

With seminar participants, Cape Town, South Africa
Photo by author.

Most of my seminars are for advanced students and practicing professionals who want to improve their skills or to refine a particular language combination. My French-English professional seminars for ATIO take place each summer in Ontario; this summer we will be at the Château Laurier in Ottawa the first week of July. I focus on French, Spanish and English for conference interpreting, but I also use a 'language neutral' approach that allows me to include other language combinations at some of my seminars (e.g. Portuguese in South Africa and Canada, Serbian and Albanian in Kosovo, and Dari and Pashto in my training of Canadian military escort interpreters). In the US as a consultant to the National Center for State Courts I evaluate French< >English oral examinations of court interpreters. For AIIC (L'association internationale des interprètes de conférence), I am participating in the AIIC delegation to the ASTM committee working to define nationwide standards for interpretation.

LMJ:	Which textbook do you use for your courses and seminars?
James N:	I use my own textbook, Interpretation Techniques and Exercises, which recently came out in its second edition. However, I also develop coursebooks and syllabi specifically tailored to the needs and language combinations of the institutions or student groups that I work with.
LMJ:	Is your knowledge of French acquired from the years you spent in Geneva, or have you lived in other French-speaking regions?
James N:	For 30 years all of my professional activity has been conducted partly in French, which is one of the UN's two working languages. I have always been drawn to the French language and French culture. It seems that I had a French ancestor in my family. Before the internet came along I kept up my French by subscribing to Les Temps Modernes and listening to short-wave radio, and I recall being moved by the eulogies of Charles de Gaulle in 1970. I studied French at the University of California and the Sorbonne but my exposure to French started in high school and later included both sides of the Atlantic. I lived in Paris while taking courses at the Sorbonne, and worked there for a year after graduating from the University of Geneva while waiting for my UN contract. I lived in Geneva and its environs (Annemasse, Haute-Savoie; Ferney-Voltaire, Ain) for two years as a student and later for five years as a UN staff member. I also spent many vacations in Bretagne and Québec, and became fairly familiar with the French spoken in la belle province. I am proud to say that my older daughter, Catherine, is perfectly bilingual.

LMJ: Do you also do translations?

James N: Yes, mainly treaties and national human rights reports for the UN in Geneva, but I have also translated legal materials for the State Department and for an international tribunal.

LMJ: You have said that residents of Québec 'know two languages for the price of one.' Give us your impressions of French spoken by the Québécois.

James N: Interpreters sometimes complain that Canadian French makes their work more difficult but I find those complaints exaggerated. The Québécois accent is at first difficult to get used to but once your ear is attuned to it you discover that the French spoken by educated Canadians is basically a regional variety of standard French with some additional dialectical features —a situation akin to that which Spanish-English interpreters face with the diverse regional varieties of Spanish in Latin America. Moreover, Canadians take official bilingualism seriously and lavish great care on making their official publications and diplomatic communications correct and elegant in both languages. At the UN, most speeches by Canadian delegates are made partly in French and what you are often hearing from them is well-written French spoken with a slight English accent. I think the language of Molière is alive and well in Canada, although it may differ from the French spoken in Paris, Marseille, Geneva or Dakar. When Nicolas Sarkozy, a brilliant speaker, was received at the Quebec National Assembly, it was hard to say who was more eloquent, the guest or the hosts. I occasionally have the pleasure of teaching French > English refresher training workshops for the staff interpreters at the Legislative Assembly of Ontario (who work mainly into French) and I am always impressed by the polished and articulate French spoken by Canadian parliamentarians and their interpreters.

Legislative Chamber – Ontario Legislative Assembly (Queens Park), Toronto. The interpreting booth is located in the corner, adjacent to the gallery.

Photo, with permission, from OLA website (https://www.ola.org/en/offices-divisions-branches/copyright)

LMJ: You have described interpreting as 'playing detective'. Could you elaborate on that in general and with specific reference to accent?

James N: I was referring to an element of my model of interpretation, on which I base my seminars; I try to identify the various processes that take place in an interpreter's mind while he is interpreting, and one of these is inference/extrapolation/deduction. What I mean is that there are many aspects of an utterance that can render it difficult to interpret, e.g. use of unfamiliar terminology, poor sound quality, conference-room noise, an inadvertent slip of the tongue or omission by the speaker, an obscure accent, etc., and in order to deal with those kinds of issues the interpreter is often obliged to go behind the words, fill in the blanks and read between the lines in order to grasp or reconstruct the speaker's meaning. This kind of analysis is very similar to what a detective does when he deduces the missing piece of the puzzle from all of the other available clues. That is why it is important for an interpreter to follow the thread of the speaker's ideas, focus on the context, and keep the overall picture in mind, rather than focusing exclusively on the words he is currently hearing.

LMJ: What direction is the profession of interpreting now taking?

James N: Like everything else, it is being changed by technology. What technology makes possible sooner or later comes to pass, and I believe we are on the verge of seeing multilingual real-time virtual meetings being convened in cyberspace using simultaneous interpretation and video-conferencing, with the speakers and the interpreters participating from different locations. For example, the Prime Minister of Japan, speaking Japanese ten thousand kilometers away in Tokyo, was brought into a conversation taking place in English in Davos, Switzerland. Due to the size of the monitor, the 'remote' participant was actually the most visible person in attendance. Just as simultaneous interpreting proved to be more efficient than consecutive, I think remote video-conference interpreting will in some cases prove to be more efficient than conference-room interpreting. Let me mention a moment of crisis that I witnessed as an interpreter and venture a prediction. I believe that in years to come the heightened security concerns that were ushered in by 9/11 will probably remain at the 'orange alert' state or higher, to use the terminology now in use at airports. I have had that feeling since September12th, 2001, when I was one of the two English interpreters called in to New York City to service the emergency meeting of the UN Security Council which met that day in response to the attack. Making my way through a deserted Manhattan where the dust was still settling from the destruction of the twin towers, I could not help wondering if the attacks were really over but I knew that despite the danger in the air the Council had to meet. I sensed that, for interpreters as for everyone else, things would never be the same again and security would become a constant concern. Remote interpreting has the potential to address not only the obstacle of geographical distance but also some security situations where high-level gatherings could become targets of terrorism. Moreover, where a meeting must be arranged on short notice or when a problem of 'rare' language combinations arises, remote interpreting can make it possible to use the best-qualified interpreters for the job even if they are remotely located and cannot be brought in time to the meeting venue. While bearing in mind that interpreters' presence at the meeting venue is always preferable because it enables interpreters to interact with the participants and be better informed, I believe that the possibilities offered by remote interpretation should also be explored.

LMJ: What advice would you give to someone embarking on a career as an interpreter?

James N: I would say: take the necessary time to thoroughly master your working languages, including your 'A' language, and to acquire the necessary background knowledge, training, and hands-on experience. Do not confine yourself solely to academic settings. An appropriate degree, such as the Master in Conference Interpreting (MCI), from a good school will help you enter the profession, but interpreting is above all an art that is learned by doing. Build a reputation for quality and reliability. If you have no experience of public speaking and suffer from stage-fright, find a way to acquire more self-confidence, e.g. by joining a public speaking club like 'Toastmasters' or an amateur theater group. Keep fit and learn to relax. Explore career possibilities with internet searches and tools like the *Yearbook of International Organizations*, which lists all international organizations in the world, indexed by subject-matter, location and working languages. Take pains with your resume. Prepare for competitive examinations using the organizations' web sites. When starting out, accept even brief volunteer assignments as a community interpreter for the sake of experience. Join an interpreter's association as a student member. Study the AIIC Code of Professional Ethics and Tips for Beginners. Read widely in all your languages and broaden your general knowledge by attending meetings or lectures on current issues. Set your goals carefully, use your time wisely, and take advantage of the opportunities that come your way. Practice interpreting daily, using the wealth of speeches now available on the internet. Record yourself, listen to your performances with a critical ear, and then work systematically on getting better at whatever gave you trouble, whether it was speed of delivery, financial terminology, metaphors, numbers, or reformulation. Resist the temptation of becoming a 'polyglutton'[166]: mastering two or three languages is better than knowing several superficially. Finally, do not spend too much time on abstract linguistic theorizing. Remember the advice of De Gaulle's interpreter, Constantin Andronikov: 'The interpreter is like a centipede; if he thought about what his feet are doing, he would be unable to walk.'

Notes

(1) Kahneman, D. (2011) *Thinking, Fast and Slow* (p. 23). London: Penguin Books.
(2) Based on a presentation made to the Twenty-Sixth Annual Conference of the Carolina Association of Translators and Interpreters (CATI) at Cape Fear Community College, Wilmington, North Carolina on 27 April 2013.
(3) Kahneman, loc. cit.
(4) Gazzaniga, M. 'The Interpreter' http://www.youtube.com/watch?v=mJKloz2vwlc
(5) *Translation as Intercultural Communication*. Professor Juliane House. Lecture at University of Macau, 28 May 2015. (emphasis supplied) https://fah.umac.mo/english/activities-english/translation-as-intercultural-communication-by-prof-juliane-house/
(6) 'One of my goals is to show that the most complex database available to any person is one's knowledge of one's native language.' Dougherty, R. *Natural Language Computing: An English Generative Grammar in Prolog* (p. xxiii). Hillsdale, New Jersey and Hove, UK: Laurence Erlbaum Associates, Publishers.
(7) Directorate-General for Translation. Studies on translation and multilingualism. Contribution of translation to the multilingual society in the EU (English summary) http://ec.europa.eu/dgs/translation/publications/studies/index_en.htm
(8) See e.g. the 'wearable translator' at https://www.facebook.com/DavidAvocadoWolfe/videos/10154225377071512/
(9) See e.g.: 'Parlez-vous Java? Sprechen Sie Python? At least four states have either passed or considered measures that would delight high school students who have trouble rolling their r's. Rather than taking Spanish to satisfy their foreign language requirement, they could take a computer language.' Bloomberg, 2 April 2015. https://www.bloomberg.com/news/articles/2015-04-02/soon-students-may-learn-to-code-instead-of-taking-french-class. See also: 'Florida Senate considers computer coding as a foreign language for high school students' http://www.miamiherald.com/news/local/education/article47876135.html
(10) *Indifference toward Foreign Languages Could Cost Americans*, posted by Marisa Sanfilippo, 2 February 2017. https://www.goodcall.com/news/foreign-languages-010001
(11) A helpful attempt to pin down this elusive distinction was made by the United States Supreme Court in its 2011 *Taniguchi* decision, which focuses on the differences between oral and written work products, their relative costs, and which party in a legal proceeding should bear those costs. https://www.supremecourt.gov/opinions/11pdf/10-1472.pdf Recent scholarly works extending the boundaries of translation beyond language per se include: Kobus Marais, A Biosemiotic Theory of Translation, Routledge 2018-10-22; Michael Cronin, Translation in the Age of the Anthropocene, Routledge 2016-11-29. A recent scholarly work on the complex role of translation in dissemination of literatures around the world is: Susan Bassenett, Translation and World Literature, Routledge 28-08-09.
(12) Kenneally, Christine. *Op. cit.*, p. 3.
(13) By estimation, the brain has about 100 million MIPS of processing power while recent super-computers only have a few million MIPS of processor speed. http://library.thinkquest.org/C001501/the_saga/compare.htm

   An informative and thorough discussion of the areas of the brain involved in simultaneous interpretation, based on recent research, may be found at: http://mosaicscience.com/story/other-words-inside-lives-and-minds-real-time-translators. The latest effort to improve MT involves models using neural networks that attempt to replicate human thought: https://slator.com/technology/google-applies-for-neural-machine-translation-patent-experts-react/. However, the results have so far been mixed: http://www.bbc.com/news/business-36638929?SThisFB&post_id=10209393538536195_10209393543576321#_=_

   See also: *Humans Triumph over Machines in Translation Competition*. Hankyoreh. 22 February 2017. http://english.hani.co.kr/arti/english_edition/e_business/783734.html and

Human Interpreter Beats Translation Program Hands Down. Chosunilbo. 22 February 2017. http://english.chosun.com/site/data/html_dir/2017/02/22/2017022201554.html

(14) Kenneally, Christine. Op. cit., p. 9.

(15) Talk with Steven Pinker at Mercatus Center, 2 November 2016. https://www.youtube.com/watch?v=CVaWR8ISEd4&feature=youtu.be

(16) It should be borne in mind that language, as defined by linguists, includes more than words and grammatical rules. It certainly includes gestures and it may be thought to include utterances and vocalizations such as laughter and crying. Kenneally, Christine. *Op, cit.*, p. 115.

(17) See: Self-Driving Uber Car Kills Pedestrian in Arizona, Where Robots Roam. *New York Times*, 19 March 2019. https://www.nytimes.com/2018/03/19/technology/uber-driverless-fatality.html

(18) Milan, J. (2012) Are smartphones intelligent enough to translate and interpret? *CATI Quarterly*, Fall/Winter.

(19) See, e.g., Beaumont, C. 'NEC unveils Tele Scouter "translation glasses",' Telegraph.co.uk, www.telegraph.co.uk/technology/news/6493869/NEC-unveils-Tele-Scouter-translation-glasses.html

(20) https://www.futura-sciences.com/tech/actualites/intelligence-artificielle-ia-traduit-livre-800-pages-12-heures-73163/

(21) Lovett Cline, B. (1965) *Men Who Made a New Physics* (p. 151). University of Chicago Press. / *Los Creadores de la Nueva Física*. Fondo de Cultura Económica, México D.F. 1973 , translation by Juan Almela. p. 201.

(22) https://www.astm.org/Standards/F2089.htm

(23) Machine Translation (MT) often performs the function of a cheat sheet, responding automatically to given stimuli with a limited range of predetermined outputs and unthinkingly generating errors that range from the absurd to the egregious, as in the two experimental drafts below, showing that MT cannot be relied upon to glean intent and nuance from context. No human would have missed nuances such as these. [Source: experimental MT drafts produced during author's translation of UN document CCPR/C/SR.2299]

EXAMPLE A: 'MR. O'FLAHERTY APPEARS IN BRACKETS' (with his proposal)

   61. M. WIERUSZEWSKI *(Rapporteur pour le Tadjikistan) dit que la proposition de M. O'Flaherty, qui apparaît entre crochets et à laquelle il souscrit sans réserve, visait à attirer l'attention des membres du Comité sur la question cruciale de l'instauration d'une coopération plus étroite..*

   MT: 61. Mr. WIERUSZEWSKI *(Rapporteur for Tajikistan) said that the proposal of Mr. O'Flaherty, who appears in brackets and that he fully endorsed, was to draw the attention of members of the Committee on the crucial issue of the establishment a closer cooperation...*

EXAMPLE B: 'PARENTS WERE CARRIED OUT' *(relatives were executed)*

   10. M. SHEARER *propose, au dernier alinéa, d'ajouter «d'urgence» avant «des mesures», pour souligner le caractère dramatique de la situation des familles qui ne savent pas quand leurs parents sont exécutés et où ils sont enterrés.*

   MT: 10. Mr. SHEARER *offers in the last paragraph, add 'emergency' before 'action', to emphasize the dramatic nature of the situation of families who do not know when their parents were carried out and where they were buried.*

See also: a recent report revealing that Artificial Intelligence programs attempting to process human language apparently lack even the elementary capacity for judgment possessed by toddlers which we refer to as 'common sense', as in the following example: 'A Winograd Schema question is one that is extremely easy for humans to answer, but defies the cold logic of computers. Take the following example: 'The man couldn't lift his son because he was so weak. Who was weak, the man or his son?' In this case, 'he' could logically refer to either the man or his son. But as humans, we know it would be silly to mention that the son was weak in this context. For computers, the 'he' is equally valid for both.' https://www.weforum.org/agenda/2016/08/why-ai-still-has-less-common-sense-than-a-toddler?utm_content=bufferb06de&utm_medium=social&utm_source=facebook.com&utm_campaign=buffer. The computer's inability to reason with empathy is shown clearly in this example.

Computers are also unable to reproduce most common emotions or moods; here is a machine translation of a traditional holiday song: https://www.facebook.com/malindakathleenreese/videos/957843254367341/

(24) Faizal Malik. *Maharashtra govt bars employees from using Google Translate.* *Hindustan Times*, 14 December 2015. http://www.hindustantimes.com/mumbai/maharashtra-govt-bars-employees-from-using-google-translate/story-TGTXYC9OLulDK6TwDLvFXJ.html]

(25) Roland, R.A. (1999) *Interpreters as Diplomats: A Diplomatic History of the Role of Interpreters in World Politics.* Ottawa, University of Ottawa Press Language itself, the instrument translators use in their work, is roughly ten times older, as the oldest known sample of recorded symbols is 300,000 years old: 'What seems to be the earliest non-utilitarian object thus far discovered comes from Pech de l'Azé in France, and has been dated to around three hundred thousand years ago.' Leakey, R. E. and Lewin, R. (1977) *Origins.* New York: E. P. Dutton.

(26) Asimov, I. (1964) Asimov, *Biographical Encyclopedia of Science and Technology* (p. 52). Garden City NY: Doubleday & Co.

(27) Aranda, L.V. (2016) *Introducción a los Estudios de Traducción* (p. 12). University Press of America, Lanham, Maryland. Translation by James Nolan. See also: https://aiic.net/page/8699

(28) Lord Kinross (1977) *The Ottoman Centuries – The Rise and Fall of the Turkish Empire* (p. 384). New York: Morrow Quill Paperbacks.

(29) A well-documented example is that of Japan. See, e.g.: 'Japan could not have attained this height of cultural advancement without outside influence. Using examples in Japan's history, it is shown that as an isolated country, Japan's cultural evolution was slower, compared to other countries where cultural diffusion played a big role in their history.' Baker, M. Cultural Diffusion and its Effects on Japan. http://www.samurai-archives.com/cde.html

(30) Northup, G.T. (1925) *An Introduction to Spanish Literature* (pp. 71–72). Chicago & London: University of Chicago, 1925. (Third edition revised and enlarged by Nicholson B. Adams.)

(31) Boorstin, D.J. (1983) *The Discoverers: A History of Man's Search to Know his World and Himself* (p. 548). New York: Random House.

(32) http://en.wikipedia.org/wiki/Ancient_Greek_medicine: '*Through long* **contact with Greek culture**, and their eventual conquest of Greece, the Romans **absorbed** many of the Greek ideas on medicine. (…) This **acceptance** led to the **spread** of Greek medical theories throughout the Roman Empire, and thus a large portion of the West. The most influential Roman scholar to continue and **expand on the Hippocratic tradition** was Galen (d. c. 207). **Study of Hippocratic and Galenic texts**, however, all but disappeared in the Latin West in the Early Middle Ages, following the collapse of the Western Empire, (…) After 750 AD, Muslim Arabs also had Galen's works in particular **translated**, and thereafter **assimilated** the Hippocratic-Galenic tradition, eventually making some of their own **expansions upon** this tradition, with the most influential being Avicenna. Beginning in the late eleventh century, the Hippocratic-Galenic tradition returned to the Latin West, with a series of **translations** of the Galenic and Hippocratic texts, mainly from Arabic **translations** but occasionally from the original Greek. In the Renaissance, more **translations** of Galen and Hippocrates directly from the Greek were made from newly available Byzantine manuscripts.' (emphasis supplied)

(33) http://blog.fxtrans.com/2013/02/is-translation-waste-of-paper.html See also note XVII.

(34) See, e.g.: reports that a computer program called 'Ross' built on the IBM cognitive computer known as 'Watson' is now functioning as an 'electronic attorney' (or, more accurately, an automated legal research engine). 'Law firm Baker & Hostetler has become the first official law firm to announce that they have hired an automated lawyer, named Ross. The firm hired Ross for their bankruptcy practice which currently employs 50 human lawyers.' http://nextshark.com/ibm-ai-ross-baker-hostetler/See also this recent article on legal automation: http://www.globallegalpost.com/big-stories/legal-automation-is-more-of-a-perception-than-reality-research-claims-77508890/

(35) 'We are forced to believe that language is an immensely ancient heritage of the human race, whether or not all forms of speech are the historical outgrowth of a single pristine form. It is doubtful if any other cultural asset of man, be it the art of drilling for fire or of chipping stone, may lay claim to a greater age. I am inclined to believe that it antedated even the lowliest developments of material culture, that these developments, in fact, were not strictly possible until language, the tool of significant expression, had itself taken shape.' [Edward Sapir, *Language: an introduction to the study of speech*, p.23]

See also the theory that development of language may have been a factor of adaptation and natural selection involved in the survival of the human species, as in the writings of Steven Pinker and Paul Boom reported by C Kenneally: 'Before they [Pinker and Bloom] launched their argument about adaptation and natural selection, the authors reiterated some important and, at the time, well-accepted facts about language. For example, as far as we know, humanity has always had language. There were no creatures that we would think of as effectively human, no highly organized societies of people that hunted, gathered and nurtured their offspring through a long period of vulnerable infancy, without language.' Kenneally, Christine. *The First Word: the search for the origins of language*. Penguin, New York, 2007. P 58.

See also a recent estimate of the origins of the indo-european languages based on computer modeling and phylogeography, which places the approximate age of these languages at 7,000 to 9,500 years: Bouckaret et al., *Mapping the Origins and Expansion of the Indo-European Language Family*, Science, 24 Aug 2012.

See also a recent (11 June 2015) DNA-based study which concludes that the Indo-European languages derive from a massive migration 4.5 to 5 thousand years ago from the Black Sea steppes: http://www.nature.com/articles/nature14317. epdf?referrer_access_token=PNyDuTBMFXSd6uv34wwVUNRgN0jAjWel9jnR3Z oTv0Pp60Qt_x2EIKCBsT-Ant7n1mUgLn_8H0CwSQ9eTgq98NqqcvwBEOaJN7Ek s2BRY_Rc2il76Kumd6knDwVqC0HdJ2PddKwxTwLp5fOvOfhdk-gqGVsA874Gs7Vb8-8xZdTm90aQHWNlCJAbPCZPo3aPYXQIBvjG2Pk-BZKhXe7IcA%3D%3D& tracking_referrer=elpais.com

(36) Roland, R.A. (1999) *Interpreters as Diplomats: A Diplomatic History of the Role of Interpreters in World Politics* (p. 9). University of Ottawa Press: 'As anthropologists know, even the most primitive of peoples maintained an intertribal communication which must be deemed an elementary form of diplomacy. But since not all tribes spoke the same language, it is certain that some of the emissaries were bilingual.'

(37) Current estimates range from 4,000 to 9,000 years: 'Linguists believe that the first speakers of the mother tongue, known as proto-Indo-European, were chariot-driving pastoralists who burst out of their homeland on the steppes above the Black Sea about 4,000 years ago and conquered Europe and Asia. A rival theory holds that, to the contrary, the first Indo-European speakers were peaceable farmers in Anatolia, now Turkey, about 9,000 years ago, who disseminated their language by the hoe, not the sword.' http://www.nytimes.com/2012/08/24/science/indo-european-languages-originated-in-anatolia-analysis-suggests.html?_r=1&src=me&ref=general&pagewanted=all

(38) The physiological feature of the human brain associated both with capacity for syntax and with the performance of complex sequences of movements such as those involved in tool-making, is the basal ganglia. Among humans in America, this feature must have evolved by about 8000 or 9000 B.C. based on archaeological evidence of complex tool-making. See: Kenneally, Christine. *The First Word: the search for the origins of language*. Penguin, New York, 2007. Pp. 74-79, and Morrison, Samuel E., *The Oxford History of the American People*. New York, Oxford University Press, 1965. p. 6.

(39) The oldest known sample of recorded symbols is 300,000 years old: 'What seems to be the earliest non-utilitarian object thus far discovered comes from Pech de l'Azé in France, and has been dated to around three hundred thousand years ago.' Leakey, R.E. and Lewin, R. (1977) *Origins*. New York: E. P. Dutton, New York.

This estimate seems corroborated in the following view by Gaia Vince: 'The first words ever uttered may have been as far back as 250,000 years ago, once our ancestors stood up on two legs and freed the ribcage from weight-bearing tasks, allowing fine nerve control of breathing and pitch to develop. And when humans had got one language, it wouldn't have been long before we had many. Language evolution can be compared to biological evolution, but whereas genetic change is driven by environmental pressures, languages change and develop through social pressures. Over time, different groups of early humans would have found themselves speaking different languages. Then, in order to communicate with other groups – for trade, travel and so on – it would have been necessary for some members of a family or band to speak other tongues.' http://mosaicscience.com/bilingual-brains

(40) See e.g McWhorter, J. (2004) *The Story of Human Language*. Chantilly VA. The Teaching Company.

(41) 'Writing is a kind of fossil and so can tell us a little about the languages that have been recorded since it was invented. While it shares a lot with spoken language, including most of its words and much organizational structure, writing cannot be considered the bare bones of speech, for it is something else entirely. Writing is static, structured by the conventions of punctuation and the use of space. The kinds of sentences that occur in writing bear only an indirect relationship to the more free-flowing and complex structures of speech. Writing has no additional channels for avoiding ambiguity, as speech has with intonation and gesture. And writing is only six thousand years old.' Kenneally, C. (2007) *The First Word: The Search for the Origins of Language*. New York: Penguin Books, New York.

(42) 'Antes del Descurbirmiento de América, dada la densa y variada población del continente, ya existían intérpretes indígenas que traducían órdenes y mandatos para hacerlos conocer entre las tribus de lenguas diferentes. Un ejemplo es la tribu de los naugatlatos, quienes eran una suerte de intérpretes oficiales de la monarquía azteca que acompañaban, de región en region, a los emisarios del Imperio para pregonar órdenes y el monto de los tributos.'—*Breve Historia de la Profesión de Traductor Público en el Río de la Plata*, in Magee, María Cristina & Pereiro, Mercedes. *Brisas de la Historia: Colegio de Traductores Públicos de la Ciudad de Buenos Aires – Profesión y Carrera*. 2008. (Historical compendium published by the Association of Public Translators of the Province of Buenos Aires).

(43) The historical novel *The Gold Eaters* by Richard Wright, (Riverhead Books; Reprint edition November 1, 2016), presents a plausible and fascinating reconstruction of how the two languages interacted with Spanish during the conquest and the role played by interpreters in that process.

(44) In March 1521, having discovered his eponymous Strait and named and sailed the Pacific, Magellan had his three remaining vessels dock at what he mistakenly believed to be the Spice Islands. Enrique did not understand anything said by any of the natives he met: they were in fact in what was to become the Philippines. He was, however, able to communicate with the rulers of the islands, as Malay was the lingua franca of

diplomacy and trade, and known to the region's elites. (...) Enrique came to negotiate for Magellan and represent the King of Spain. On Good Friday, 1521, he arranged for the rajah of the island of Limasawa to send fish and rice to the ships. (...) Enrique was also involved in converting the ruler and his brother to Catholicism. He played a key role in similar dealings with Rajah Humabon of Cebu. —Adams, Christine. *Looking for Interpreter Zero: (2) Enrique, Magellan's Slave Interpreter.* in AIIC blog http://extranet.aiic.net/page/6387

(45) See: review of *Interpreters with Lewis and Clark. The Story of Sacagawea and Toussaint Charbonneau,* by W. Dale Nelson at http://www.le-mot-juste-en-anglais.com/2016/07/interpreters-with-lewis-and-clark-the-story-of-sacagawea-and-toussaint-charbonneau-by-w-dale-nelson.html

(46) Excerpt from a review of: Ruth A. Roland. *Interpreters as Diplomats: A Diplomatic History of the Role of Interpreters in World Politics* (Ottawa, University of Ottawa Press, 1999, 209 p.) by Ian Martin, English Department, Glendon College, York University. URL: http://id.erudit.org/iderudit/006810ar

(47) Holt, P.M., Lambton, A.K.S. and Lewis B. (Eds) (1970) *The Cambridge History of Islam.* Cambridge University Press. Opensource Collection. Pp. 581 – 582 https://archive.org/details/CambridgeHistoryOfIslamVol2B

(48) Summarized from: Baught, A.C. (1935) *A History of the English Language* (p. 2). New York: Appleton-Century-Crofts. See also: Wogan-Browne, Jocelyn. The English Language Is, and Was, Profoundly Multicultucultural. The Public Medievalist, 19 December 2019. https://www.publicmedievalist.com/multicultural-english/?fbclid=IwAR3Llc66lhSpCLFJuway7pFl1-0A2dPemsBATu2HyTEBeGq12-p-81YnQgk Another major world language, Spanish, presents a similar historical mosaic of Roman, Germanic, Arabic and other influences.

(49) Interview with David Crystal at Edinburgh International Book Festival, 18 May 2016. https://www.youtube.com/watch?v=w6tZYVNG8OI&feature=share

(50) Boorstin, D.J. (1983) *The Discoverers: A History of Man's Search to Know his World and Himself* (p. 548). New York: Random House.

(51) http://en.wikipedia.org/wiki/Latin_influence_in_English

(52) English is the mother language of an estimated 341 million people and the second language of 508 million people in over sixty countries. Site for Language Management in Canada. https://slmc.uottawa.ca/?q=english_world_status

(53) It is wise to remember, in this regard, that English is only one of three dominant or pre-eminent languages that have been used as a global common language during the recorded history of international relations and may not be the last. Professor Dietrich Kappeler, former director of the Mediterranean Academy of Diplomatic Studies, summarizes the history of language use in diplomacy as follows: 'Documents exchanged between countries in the past were written in the single vehicular language then in use in Europe: Latin. In the 18th century French had become the generally accepted diplomatic language, so much so that even diplomatic notes addressed to the British Foreign Office by the Legation of the USA were written in that language. The 20th century saw a gradual emergence of English as a second and later even dominant diplomatic language. At the same time, a growing number of countries insisted on the use of their own language in diplomatic correspondence and joint diplomatic documents. As a result the United Nations admitted to five languages at its inception (Chinese, English, French, Russian and Spanish), to which Arabic has later been added by informal agreement. In the European Union, all twelve languages of the members are currently in use and their number is bound to grow as new members will be admitted. Translation and interpretation have therefore become a major element in present-day diplomatic life.' *Texts in Diplomacy*, Language and Diplomacy, Malta: DiploProjects, 2001, cited in website *Diplo* at http://www.diplomacy.edu/language/translation

(54) Gaiba, F. (1998) *The Origins of Simultaneous Interpretation: The Nuremberg Trial.* Ottawa: University of Ottawa Press. See also the story of Colonel Leon Dostert: https://sfs.georgetown.edu/chief-interpreter-nuremberg-trials-leaves-mark-georgetown/

(55) The film 'The Interpreters: A Historical Perspective' was produced by Evelyn Moggio-Ortiz, Executive Producer and creator, for the Oral History Project for the UN 50th Anniversary. Ms. Moggio-Ortiz formed a Working Group composed of fellow UN staff interpreters representing the UN's six official languages, in which the author participated as a member.

(56) Baigorri-Jalón, J. (2004) *Interpreters at the United Nations: A History* (p. 60). Salamanca, Ediciones Universidad.

(57) Ibid., pp. 60–61.

(58) Survey on Expectations of Users of Conference Interpretation, January 1995, International Association of Conference Interpreters, p. 11.

(59) Ibid, p. 12 (emphasis supplied)

(60) Former Director of the Graduate Institute of Translation and Interpretation Studies of Fu Jen University, Taiwan.

(61) Setton, R. *Training conference interpreters*, article published on the web site of Conference Interpreters Asia Pacific (CIAP), www.ciap.net

(62) *Europarl* : www.europarl.eu.int/interp/public/confint/confint_en.htm

(63) See e.g. http://www.unlanguage.org/UNTraining/Schools/default.aspx

(64) See: http://ec.europa.eu/dgs/scic/docs/cooperation/list_universities_europa.pdf

(65) Pullum. G. (2016) The social consequences of switching to English. *The Chronicle of Higher Education.* 20 April 2016.

(66) Albright, M. (2003) *Madam Secretary, A Memoir* (p. 254). New York: Hyperion.

(67) Fisher, R.; Ury, W. and Patton, B. (1981) *Getting to Yes.* Penguin.

(68) While the six UN official languages are the first or second language of less than half of the world's population (2.8 billion people), they are official languages in more than half the nations of the world.

(69) See: The United Nations Convention on the Law of the Sea; A Historical Perspective, at: http://www.un.org/Depts/los/convention_agreements/convention_historical_perspective.htm

See also Chronological list of ratifications, at: http://www.un.org/depts/los/reference_files/chronological_lists_of_ratifications.htm

(70) *Staffing and Foreign Language Shortfalls Persist Despite Initiatives to Address Gaps,* GAO-06-894, August 2006, pp. 28 and 31, cited in: Summary Review of Public Diplomacy Efforts - Report Number ISP-I-07-08, June 2007, page 16.

(71) See e.g. Nolan, J. (2005) *Interpretation Techniques and Exercises* (pp. 63–64). Clevedon: Multilingual Matters.

(72) See, e.g. Korchilov, I. (1997) *Translating History.* New York: Scribner.

(73) Cremona, V.A. and Helena Mallia, H. (2001) In J. Kurbalija and H. Slavik (eds) *Interpretation and Diplomacy.* Language and Diplomacy.

(74) Korchilov, I. (1997) *Translating History* (pp. 166–167). New York: Scribner.

(75) Regarding the importance of the personal relationships that are formed between the diplomatic interpreter and his principals, and the insight he gains from his dealings with them, see two excellent recent memoirs: Korchilov, I. (1997) *Translating History.* New York: Scribner and Obst, H. (2010) *White House Interpreter: The Art of Interpretation.* Bloomington: Author House. See also the recollections of Pavel Palazhennko, former interpreter to Mikhail Gorbachev, in this online interview: *US-Russia relations declining but past achievements are never in vain:* https://www.rt.com/shows/sophieco/448537-gorbachev-interpreter-us-russia/?fbclid=IwAR3uqoO5uRJ1DLQvWK4osi_nwgbuEB2IZiFxis52xkiLpSeA-L7L0YndtX4

(76) '...it was clear that the two leaders had decided to jettison all personal, bureaucratic, and diplomatic baggage to focus on elevating the overused expression of the underachieving 'strategic partnership.' *Times of India*, 1 October 2014. http://timesofindia.

indiatimes.com/india/Modi-Obama-meet-India-and-US-will-jointly-take-on-terror-take-off-for-Mars/articleshow/43933307.cms

(77) http://www.ethnologue.com/world

(78) See: 'Supreme Court says Alberta doesn't have to make its laws in both English and French.' National Post, 20 November 2015. http://nationalpost.com/news/canada/supreme-court-says-alberta-doesnt-have-to-make-its-laws-in-both-english-and-french

(79) This is in line with the international law distinction between *acta jure imperii* and *acta jure gestionis* or, roughly speaking, sovereign acts and commercial acts of states.

(80) The decision of the United Kingdom in June of 2016 to withdraw from the European Union prompted speculation that English would be dropped from the EU's official languages. The author argued against this idea in the following article: http://www.irishlegal.com/4673/blog-brexit-and-standard-english/, reproduced in Chapter VIII of this volume. It seems, however, that some form of status quo will be retained for the foreseeable future: 'At her press conference at the close of the two-day EU summit in Brussels, Ms May was asked if she considered the idea of conducting talks in French as 'a gesture of good intent'. Ducking the question, she replied simply: 'We will conduct the negotiations in the way that is going to make sure that we get the right deal for the United Kingdom.' Meanwhile, German Chancellor Angela Merkel said there was no official language for the Brexit talks and that 'we are all entitled to speak in our native tongue'. http://www.independent.co.uk/news/uk/politics/brexit-negoti-ations-french-theresa-may-eu-leaders-row-a7374251.html

(81) See, e.g. United Nations language services: https://languagecareers.un.org/dgacm/Langs.nsf/home.xsp

(82) *L'Interprétation de conférence face à l'élargissement, une stratégie pour le SCIC à l'horizon 2004*, European Commission, SEC (2002) 349/22, p. 8.

(83) See: https://circabc.europa.eu/faces/jsp/extension/wai/navigation/container.jsp

(84) United Nations General Assembly, Official Records, A/Res./50/11, A/54/478, A/RES/54/64, ST/IC/2000/86, A/56/656.

(85) United Nations General Assembly, Official Records, A/Res./50/11, 15 November 1995 (emphasis supplied).

(86) United Nations General Assembly Official Records, A/54/478, 19 October 1999, *Multilingualism: Report of the Secretary General*.

(87) United Nations General Assembly Official Records, A/Res./54/64, 21 January 2000, *Multilingualism*.

(88) United Nations General Assembly Official Records, A/56/656, *Multilingualism: Report of the Secretary General*, 27 November 2001.

(89) International Tribunal for the Law of the Sea, *In the M/V Saiga (No. 2)*, Public hearing, March 1999. Testimony of Mr. Djibril Niasse, interpreted into French by Mr. Edaly Gassama.

(90) 'Every language, dialect, patois or lingo is a structurally complete framework into which can be poured any subtlety of emotion or thought that its users are capable of expressing. Whatever it lacks at any given time or place in the way of vocabulary and syntax can be supplied in very short order by borrowing and imitation from other languages.' Haugen, Einar. '*The Curse of Babel*' in Crawford, James ed., *Language Loyalties: a Source Book on the Official English Controversy*. Chicago & London, University of Chicago Press, 1992. p. 408.

(91) International Annual Meeting on Language Arrangements, Documentation and Publications (formerly known as the Inter-Agency Meeting on Language Arrangements, Documentation and Publications). See: https://www.iamladp.org/

(92) http://europa.eu.int/comm/scic/interpreter/iamladp_en.htm#

(93) See: https://www.iamladp.org/
    'IAMLADP meets annually under the chairmanship of the United Nations Under-Secretary-General for General Assembly and Conference Management. The annual meetings are hosted by a member organization and, since 2001, are co-chaired by the

host organization's counterpart. Currently, the rotation pattern for hosting an annual meeting is as follows: a UN duty station (New York, Geneva, Nairobi, Vienna), followed by a UN system organization, and then a non-UN system organization.

The 2019 Annual Meeting was co-hosted by the two linguistic services of the European Parliament (DG LINC and DG TRAD) and the European Commission (DG SCIC and DGT), with the support of the Translation Service of the General Secretariat of the Council of the European Union and the Directorate-General for Multilingualism of the Court of Justice of the European Union (DG TRAD and CJEU-DI), in Brussels on 27-29 May 2019. The 2020 Annual Meeting will be hosted by the United Nations Office at Nairobi.

The Brussels Statement on multilingualism, issued as an outcome of IAMLADP 2019, is available in all twenty-four official languages of the European Union (host of IAMLADP 2019) and the six official languages of the United Nations in English and French compilations.'

(94) https://www.scoop.it/t/translation-world/p/4055746004/2015/11/24/no-snub-pnoy-lack-of-translator-prevented-conversation-with-xi

(95) Source: http://www.unog.ch

(96) See the articles Dörte Andres, *Consecutive interpreting* and Ebru Diriker, *Simultaneous interpreting* in Franz Pöchhacker, Ed., Routledge *Encyclopedia of Interpreting Studies*. Routledge, London and New York, 2015.

(97) For a fairly accurate description of how a multilingual conference system is organized, see: Bellos, D. (2011) Is *That a Fish in Your Ear?* New York: Faber and Faber, New York, especially pp. 259–272, in particular the schematic on p. 267.

(98) Nolan, J. '*Educational and Technological Challenges Facing Language Services of Inter-Governmental Organizations*', presentation to the Annual General Meeting of the Canadian Language Industries Association (AILIA), Ottawa, 21 September 2004.

(99) See: Prisca Chaoui, United Nations Office at Geneva, *Distance interpreting and its challenges*. UN Special, August 2018. https://www.unspecial.org/2018/07/distance-interpreting-and-its-challenges/

(100) Video Remote Interpreting (VRI) is now in use in the new courtroom at the International Criminal Court in the Hague to receive testimony from remotely located witnesses. As recently noted in this comment from one interpreter, there seem to remain some bugs to be worked out in the audio delivery system: 'It is not always a picnic. Sometimes we hear testimony from witnesses in faraway places via videolink. And despite our AV technicians' heroic efforts (they really do all they possibly can for us), the sound quality can be .... let's say, a challenge.' Training in remote interpreting is now being included in the interpreter training program of the University of Mons: See 'L'UMons crée la visio-interprétation', *Le Soir*, Belgium, 11 June 2011. http://archives.lesoir.be/l-8217-umons-cree-la-visio-interpretation_t-20110611-01FGRD.html

(101) Based on a presentation to the New York Circle of Translators, 3 December 2005.

(102) Based on an article the author published in the *ATA Chronicle*, journal of the American Translators' Association, in July, 2010.

(103) Fraser, G. 'Our High Court Should be Bilingual,' posted April 23, 2010 by the editor of the National Post, http://network.nationalpost.com/NP/blogs/full comment/archive/2010/04/23/graham-fraser-our-high-court-should- be-bilingual.aspx

(104) http://ec.europa.eu/dgs/translation/translating/officiallanguages/index_en.htm

(105) See e.g.: (a) 'Simultaneous translation by computers will put courtroom interpreters out of a job 'within a few years' the lord chief justice has said in an upbeat assessment on the potential of technology. Delivering the Sir Henry Brooke Annual Lecture on 'the age of reform' Lord Burnett of Maldon described artificial intelligence as the 'transformative technology of our age' which would drive change in the justice system long after the current controversial reform programme ends in five years.' Michael Cross and John Hyde. Computers Will Make Interpreters Obsolete,

Lord Chief Predicts. *The Law Society Gazette*, United Kingdom, 8 June 2018. https://www.lawgazette.co.uk/practice/computers-will-make-interpreters-obsolete-lord-chief-predicts/5066416.article; (b) Beaumont, Claudia. 'NEC Unveils Tele Scouter 'Translation Glasses.' Lawson, Stephen. 'Real-Time Voice Translation Coming to Mobile.' PC World , April 22, 2010 https://www.pcworld.com/article/194847/article.html; (c) For a balanced and perceptive review of machine translation developments, see: Bellos, David. 'I, Translator.' The New York Times (March 21, 2010), www.nytimes.com/2010/03/21/opinion/21bellos.htm

(106) Nolan, J. (2005) *Interpretation Techniques and Exercises* (pp. 65–66). Clevedon: Multilingual Matters.

(107) In the simultaneous mode, certain ideas, e.g. measurements and orders of magnitude, can be more precisely expressed in a sign language than in a spoken language, which is bound by the limits of its verbal lexicon. A fifth mode of interpreting, which could be termed "delayed simultaneous", has reportedly been tried out experimentally by court interpreters John Lombardi (2003) and Erik Camayd-Freixas (2005). It consists of using the instant replay function of a digital recorder to immediately replay and interpret a speaker's full statement as soon as he has finished it. This interpretation is reportedly more faithful to the original regarding intonation and liveliness and the interpreter can listen more attentively to the speaker since he is not taking notes. Tosenberger, Tea. *Development of note-taking systems for consecutive interpreting.* Sveučilište J.J. Strossmayera u Osijeku. Filozofski fakultet. Diplomski studij engleskog i njemačkog jezika, prevoditeljski smjer. 2013.

(108) Schüler, D. (2016) *Liberating Voices: A Pattern Language for Communication Revolution*, p. 149, © 2016 by the Massachusetts Institute of Technology, reprinted courtesy of the MIT Press.

(109) Schuler, Do. op. cit.

(110) For an interesting and insightful personal account of how this intuitive process comes into play, see: Magalhães, E. 'How Do You Do That?' Translated from the original Portuguese by Barry S. Olsen. The ATA Chronicle (April 2010), 12. See also related observations in: Setton, Robin. Training Conference Interpreters (Conference Interpreters Asia Pacific), www.ciap.net/web pages/news06.html

(111) Canon 2, New Jersey Code of Professional Conduct for Interpreters, Transliterators and Translators, www.judiciary.state.nj.us/interpreters/codepub.htm.

(112) '...Ich habe mich des geflissen im Dolmetschen, dass ich rein und klar Deutsch geben möchte. Und ist uns oft begegnet, dass wir vierzehn Tage, drei, vier Wochen haben ein einziges Wort gesucht...' In Send- brief vom Dolmetschen (1530). Vogt-Lüerssen, Maike. Martin Luther in Wort und Bild (Die Deutsche Bibliothek, 2003), 50.

(113) e.g. over $3,700 per second: $112,000 being the average cost for 30 seconds of commercial prime time in broadcast TV (in 2012; up from $110,00 in 2013). http://adage.com/article/news/costs-ad-prices-tv-mobile-billboards/297928/

(114) Nafá Waasaf, María Lourdes. 'La competencia retórica en las clases de interpretación de lenguas: una propuesta didáctica basada en dis- cursos politicos parlamentarios'. (Research Papers, Consortium for the Training of Translation Teachers, 2003), 18-22, http://isg.urv.es/cttt/cttt/research.html.

(115) The language we use may even shape the way we think in fundamental ways. See, e.g.: Lera Boroditsky. How language shapes the way we think. Ted Talks, 2 May 2018. https://youtu.be/RKK7wGAYP6k

(116) The interpreter's grasp of the source language message depends on short- term memory, but his target language rendition also draws on long-term memory, that is, knowledge of the vocabulary and culture of the source and target languages.

(117) On avoidance of stereotypes in multicultural settings, see: Nolan, J. op. cit., 169–72.

(118) In this regard, see: Mikkelson, H. *"'Verbatim Interpretation" Revisited.'* Proteus (National Association of Judiciary Interpreters and Translators, Spring 2010, Volume XIX, No. 1).

(119) Albright, M. (2003) *Madam Secretary* (p. 83). New York: Miramax Books.

(120) Similarly, a sign language interpreter sometimes translates oral nuance or tone by gestures or facial expressions. See the news reports about Licya Callis reproduced below.

(121) *'The Magical Number Seven, Plus or Minus Two: Some Limits on Our Capacity for Processing Information*' is one of the most highly cited papers in psychology. It was published in 1956 by the cognitive psychologist George A. Miller of Princeton University's Department of Psychology in *Psychological Review*. It is often interpreted to argue that the number of objects an average human can hold in working memory is 7 ± 2. This is frequently referred to as *Miller's Law*. Wikipedia: https://en.wikipedia.org/wiki/The_Magical_Number_Seven,_Plus_or_Minus_Two

(122) Some moods or states of mind, such as surprise, irony or exasperation, can be expressed either verbally or gesturally in the source language and rendered either way in the target language. An interpreter working from a non-visible position should try to express these to the audience by tone and intonation. A useful discussion of gestural language is given at https://www.theguardian.com/commentisfree/2018/nov/30/v-sign-digital-message-baroness-trumpington?fbclid=IwAR1jvB4Ic1YEw2W8Hmves1izROZoY-DUMjl3z4_zUXBpKzwNktgtLCnC0KI

    For a humorous but very apt illustration of gestural language used in consecutive interpretation to accompany the spoken meaning, see: https://www.dailymotion.com/video/x186ihw

(123) For example, the White House issued a correction of an interpreted statement by President Barack Obama during a joint press conference with Prime Minister Abe of Japan to clarify that a word which had been rendered into Japanese with the meaning of 'remorse' should have been rendered with the meaning of 'regret.' See lecture by Professor Tsuruta Chikako: https://www.youtube.com/watch?v=M5arpW6YYxk

(124) See also the coping tactics suggested in the following article: http://ewandro.com/5-essential-coping-tactics/

(125) *Meet the men and women interpreting for the world's most powerful people*, Bill Birtles, China Correspondent, ABC News, Australia, 2 January 2019. https://www.abc.net.au/news/2018-12-31/chinese-interpreters-reveal-what-the-high-pressure-job-is-like/10667258?pfmredir=sm&_scpsug=crawled%2C53670%2Cen_7d0b127660fb06d6c96f134e7a17b242f5d8d30e4d471c2b61a616a921a35b49&fbclid=IwAR3Eg5_bI5kNVWSr2luzPfy2f1h1ChOsyeKmt3MhBKAN-JrITIGgjO0KgTw#_scpsug=crawled,53670,en_7d0b127660fb06d6c96f134e7a17b242f5d8d30e4d471c2b61a616a921a35b49

(126) Hagen, U. (1991) *A Challenge for the Actor* (p. 39). New York: Scribner.

(127) See, e.g.: http://www.cbc.ca/beta/news/world/un-interpretor-1.3760725 Gauging the quality of interpretation also requires one to consider whether the original speech made sense; see, e.g. *Japan's interpreters struggle to make sense of 'Trumpese'*, by Tomohiro Osaki, Japan Times, 17 February 2017 http://www.japantimes.co.jp/news/2017/02/17/national/japans-interpreters-struggle-to-make-sense-of-trump-speeches/#.WMhVwU3rseg

(128) See, e.g., this example: https://www.facebook.com/Fox4DFW/videos/1923196171132216/UzpfSTEwNTE3Njc4NjU6MTAyMTQ0MTQ1NTE1MzE1NjQ/

(129) Kenneally, C. (2007) *The First Word – The Search for the Origins of Language*. New York: Penguin Books.

(130) For example, the rule applying to freelance interpreters at the European Union provides that they 'shall be bound by the strictest secrecy, which shall be observed towards all persons and with regard to all information disclosed in the course of the practice of the profession at any gathering not open to the public.'

(131) Full text available at www.calliope-interpreters.org/news-and-articles/how-remote-should-interpretation-be, accessed on. Copyright ©Calliope-Interpreters 2018. Calliope-Interpreters is a global network of AIIC Consultant Interpreters.] Reproduced by permission. During public health emergencies, appropriate precautions should also be considered when organizing interpreting services for large public gatherings so that remote interpreting enables social distancing: https://aiic.net/page/8956/

(132) http://www.astm.org/Standards/F2089.htm

(133) John Clare ed., *Captured in Time: Five Centuries of South African Writing.* Reproduced by courtesy of Jonathan Ball Publishers, Johannesburg & Cape Town, 2010. Page 386. Reproduced by permission of the publisher.

(134) Maalouf, Amin (1984) *The Crusades through Arab Eyes* (p. 213). New York: Shocken Books, New York.

(135) Similarly, 'the language barrier' was sometimes used as a delaying tactic by defendants at the Nuremberg trial. Robert Hedrick, a US attorney and an Adjunct Professor at Seattle University, an avid student of the Trials, delivered a PowerPoint presentation, '*From History's Greatest Trial: The Cross-Examination of Hermann Goering*,' to audiences in the US and Australia. ... Mr Hedrick said that some people believed the O. J. Simpson case was the trial of the century but he was clear that the description belonged 'hands down' to Nuremberg. Sometimes the delaying tactic took the form of ostensible complaints about translations of questions:
   'We had the most significant Nazi who survived the War, Hermann Goering, and more than 20 others...it brought out some great performances and some not-so-great performances by the lawyers involved,' he said. The US Supreme Court Justice Robert Jackson was the lead prosecutor for the US, and his cross-examination of Goering lasted two-and-a-half days, and was followed by another half day by David Maxwell Fyfe, of Britain's prosecution team. Mr Hedrick said Goering was a 'slippery' witness, who often complained about the translation of questions to buy time to think of an answer.' [http://www.scottishlegal.com/2016/05/20/advocates-given-glimpse-into-history-of-nuremberg-trials/]

(136) Glenny, M. (1996) *The Fall of Yugoslavia, the Third Balkan War.* London: Penguin Books.

(137) Ramsey Clark *et al.* (1992) *War Crimes: A Report on US War Crimes Against Iraq* (p. 255). Washington DC: Maisonneuve Press.

(138) Mason, P. (1972) *Constitutional History of California* (p. 88). California Legislature, Assembly.

(139) http://barryrmccain.blogspot.com/2015/07/billy-kid-was-gaelic-speaker.html

(140) Bolton, H.E. (1949) *Coronado, Knight of Pueblos ad Plains* (p. 2). Albuquerque: The University of New Mexico Press.

(141) Muscatine, D. (1975) *Old San Francisco: The Biography of a City* (p. 31). New York: G. Putnam's Sons.

(142) Salinger, P. (1966) *With Kennedy.* New York: Doubleday.

(143) Buckley, W.F. Jr. (1974) *United Nations Journal.* (p. 62). New York: G. P. Putnam's Sons, New York.

(144) Buckley, W.F., Jr. (1974) *United Nations Journal* (pp. 133–134). New York: G. P. Putnam's Sons.

(145) Sampson, A. (1975) *The Seven Sisters* (p. 3). New York: Viking.

(146) Albright, M. (2003) *Madam Secretary, A Memoir* (p. 198). New York: Hyperion, New York.

(147) Sampson, A. (1975) *The Seven Sisters* (p. 64). New York: Viking.

(148) Polizzotti, M. (2018) Why Mistranslation Matters. *The New York Review of Books.* 28 July 2018.

(149) Murphy, R. (1964) *Diplomat Among Warriors* (p. 254). New York: Doubleday, New York. Online version available at: file:///C:/Users/HP-User/Downloads/Diplomat_Among_Warriors-Robert_Murphy-1964-497pgs-POL.sml.pdf

(150) Excerpt from *Witness to Nuremberg* by Richard Sonnenfeldt, in '*Richard Sonnenfeldt, The Jewish Interpreter At Nuremberg*' by Deborah Katz. Jewish Press, 21 November 2018. http://www.jewishpress.com/indepth/interviews-and-profiles/richard-sonnenfeldt-the-jewish-interpreter-at-nuremberg/2018/11/21/?fbclid=IwAR03RZpcsUrdazHaWXsCzHbUoLWPXu1E57oXA8yIPDPnFLy533uL11MXJ9U

(151) Brouwer, N. 'Translators are servants but they need not be servile', Babel No.2 1972 Vol. XVIII, p. 3 (emphasis added).

(152) Hazel Mae Pan, China's 'The Interpreter' Breaks 100 Million Viewer Mark in One Week. Slator, 31 May 2016. https://slator.com/industry-news/chinas-the-interpreter-breaks-100-million-viewer-mark-in-one-week/

(153) See e.g. 'В центре сердца нашей Родины на всеобщем обозрении лежит мумия коммуниста- террориста по кличке 'ленин'. Предлагаю прекратить это похоронное шоу, капище-мавзолей снести, а тело В.И.Ульянова предать земле, что более соответствует нашим духовным традициям.' [http://vk.com/club2977084].

(154) See: Korchilov, I. (1997) *Translating History: Thirty years on the Front Lines of Diplomacy with a Top Russian Interpreter* (pp. 343–344). New York: Scibner.

(155) United Nations Organization Stabilization Mission in the Democratic Republic of the Congo.

(156) *The Use of the Language Assistant in UN Peace Missions - Benefits And Risks* , By Israel Alves de Souza Júnior (Captain of the Technical Branch (QCO, acronym in Portuguese) of the Brazilian Army, professor, translator, interpreter and coordinator of the Military Translators and Interpreters Course (ETIMIL, acronym in Portuguese) of the Brazilian Peace Operations Joint Training Center (CCOPAB, acronym in Portuguese). In 2012, designated Chief of the Interpreters Section of the Brazilian Engineering Company (BRAENGCOY) in the United Nations Stabilization Mission in Haiti (MINUSTAH). Contact: oficialisrael@gmail.com) Pages 17–18. Reproduced by permission of the author.

(157) Montanelli, Indro (1969) *Historia de Roma* (p. 59). Barcelona: Ediciones G.P. (Translation by James Nolan).

(158) Boorstin, D.J. (1983) *The Discoverers: A History of Man's Search to Know his World and Himself* (pp. 548–549). New York: Random House.

(159) 'I don't speak Arabic': John Bolton says he won't listen to tape of Khashoggi killing because he won't understand it, by Jason Lemon. Newsweek, November 27, 2018. https://www.newsweek.com/john-bolton-arabic-khashoggi-killing-tape-1233893?fbclid=IwAR2j8T3ss3rKCZVJym2YTQzPiMTBKrfENEv04C6aifT8Q8vORmxy-_uPASM

(160) https://www.brainyquote.com/quotes/walt_whitman_146893?src=t_english_language

(161) Eco (1993). Quoted by Marta Alina in *Multilingualism in the European Union*. http://termcoord.eu/2018/05/multilingualism-in-the-european-union/

(162) James Nolan, J.D., AIIC, ACI, has served as Deputy Director of the Interpretation, Meetings and Publishing Division of the United Nations, Head of Linguistic and Conference Services of the International Tribunal for the Law of the Sea, Chief of the UN Verbatim Reporting Service, and UN Senior Interpreter.

(163) http://www.politico.eu/article/english-will-not-be-an-official-eu-language-after-brexit-senior-mep

(164) A possible alternative resolution of the situation would be the emergence of an independent Scotland with English as its official language. See: https://www.theguardian.com/uk-news/2017/mar/14/spain-independent-scotland-would-be-at-the-back-of-eu-queue

(165) Quotation from the book, *A Challenge for the Actor* © 1991 by Uta Hagen. p. 39. HB Studio. Training and practice for the theatre since 1945. www.UtaHagen.com and www.hbstudio.org.

(166) Also known as a 'hyperpolyglot'. See, e.g.: https://www.newyorker.com/magazine/2018/09/03/the-mystery-of-people-who-speak-dozens-of-languages?mbid=social_facebook

Index

Note: n refers to notes.